3—

GARDEN ART

Delightful Projects for a Beautiful Outdoor Space

GARDEN ART

Delightful Projects for a Beautiful Outdoor Space

Mickey Baskett

Sterling Publishing Co., Inc.
New York

Prolific Impressions Production Staff:

Editor in Chief: Mickey Baskett
Copy Editor: Phyllis Mueller
Graphics: Dianne Miller, Karen Turpin
Styling: Kirsten Jones
Photography: Jerry Mucklow
Administration: Jim Baskett

Library of Congress Cataloging-in-Publication Data

Baskett, Mickey.
  Garden art : delightful projects for a beautiful outdoor space /
Mickey Baskett.
    p. cm.
  Includes index.
  ISBN 1-4027-0343-0
  1. Garden ornaments and furniture. 2. Handicraft. I. Title.
SB473.5 .B37 2003
684.1'8--dc22

2003020844

10 9 8 7 6 5 4 3 2 1

Published by Sterling Publishing Co., Inc.
387 Park Avenue South, New York, N.Y. 10016

© 2004 by Prolific Impressions, Inc.

Produced by Prolific Impressions, Inc.
160 South Candler St., Decatur, GA 30030

Distributed in Canada by Sterling Publishing
c/o Canadian Manda Group, One Atlantic Avenue, Suite 105
Toronto, Ontario, Canada M6K 3E7
Distributed in Great Britain by Chrysalis Books Group PLC,
The Chrysalis Building, Bramley Road, London W10 6 SP, England.
Distributed in Australia by Capricorn Link (Australia) Pty. Ltd.
P.O. Box 704, Windsor, NSW 2756 Australia

Printed in China
All rights reserved
Sterling ISBN 1-4027-0343-0

Acknowledgements

Special thanks to the following manufacturers for supplying products to create the projects in this book.

For FolkArt Acrylic Colors, FolkArt Outdoor Sealer, Mod Podge Sealer/Finish, Decorator Products Durable Colors, and Paint for Plastic:
Plaid Enterprises
3225 Westech Drive
Norcross, GA 30092
www.plaidonline.com

For paint brushes:
Silver Brush Limited
P. O. Box 414
Windsor, N.J. 08561-4888
609-443-4900
www.silverbrush.com

For two-part pour-on resin:
Environmental Technologies Inc.
www.eti-usa.com

For Premo! polymer clay:
Polyform Products Co.
www.sculpey.com

Table of Contents

Nothing can calm me like going outside and sitting in my garden among nature's beauty as well as some beautiful art I have acquired and displayed in my garden. I can breathe in the fresh

air, feel the gentle breezes and listen to the tinkling of my wind chimes as they harmonize with the chirping birds. A smile relaxes my face as my eyes catch a glimpse of my whimsical angel birdfeeder that sits among my beloved hydrangeas. My breathing gets deeper and more relaxed as I contemplate my manmade pieces of art that are at home among God's beautiful gifts of nature.

Garden art may sound like guilding the lily. When gardens are so beautiful why do we need more beauty? Are we trying to compete with nature just a little? Or maybe we are trying to tame nature and fit into it a little more. Or maybe we are trying to make our attempts at art a little prettier by placing the art among some real beauties. In my opinion, Auguste Rodin's sculptures at the Paris Rodin Museum are not nearly as beautiful inside the building as those that are outside placed among the grandness of nature. The Brookgreen Garden in Pawley's Island, South Carolina contains acres of sculptural art. These gardens are magnificent. I am not sure whether the gardens are so pretty because of the sculptures or the sculptures are so pretty because of the beautiful gardens. Nevertheless, I know that gardens can be enhanced with a focal point piece of art. And art can look even more beautiful when placed in a lovely setting.

The garden art in this book contains many items that can be painted, some that can be created with a mosaics technique, and some items that are fun to construct from wood. Some of the art is whimsical and will bring a smile; some of the art has a country style appeal; all of the pieces are beautiful and creative. I hope you will be enticed to spend many delightful hours creating lovely enhancements for your garden. ❑

PAINTED GARDEN ART

Paint is the universal language of art. Paint has staying power. I am not just talking about painted items being able to withstand years of weathering in your garden – I am talking history. Paint has been around for centuries. Artists progressed quickly from rubbing a piece of burned charcoal on a stone wall to making their own paint colors from plants. From the first stroke of color on a piece of pottery or a warrior's face, there has been no stopping the progress of art. Paint can be used on wood, plastic, terra cotta, cement, slate, metal, and even glass. All of these surface materials can be used to create art for your garden.

Pictured at right: Birdhouses in a Row Potting Bench.
See page 14 for instructions.

Supplies

■ Paint

Indoor/Outdoor Acrylic Gloss Enamels

Indoor/outdoor gloss enamels are water-based, weather-resistant and durable paints that come in a variety of ready-mixed shades. They dry to a glossy sheen and can be used outdoors without a protective finish.

Acrylic Craft Paint

Acrylic craft paints are richly pigmented paints that come ready to use, usually in plastic squeeze bottles. They are available in a huge range of pre-mixed colors, including rich metallics, glitters, and sparkles. Use them as base paints and for painting designs. After painting, a protective finish is necessary for durability.

■ Paint for Plastic

Paints specifically formulated for painting on plastic are available at crafts and hardware stores in brush-on and spray forms. They're great for outdoor projects and typically are available in a range of colors that include traditionals, brights, metallics, and neons.

Some paints for plastic are waterbase and non-toxic; read labels carefully and choose the paint that meets your needs. Some paint lines include a primer that helps paint adhere to plastic and a sealer that increases durability.

■ Surfaces

Many types of surfaces are suitable for outdoor use, and the projects in this book include a variety of choices – from **wood** and **plastic** furniture and accessories like trays, birdhouses, signs, planters, and fences. There are **metal** surfaces, too – watering cans, dustpans, buckets, and lanterns, plus copper sconces you can construct from copper sheeting.

You'll find painted **concrete** stepping stones and a **cement** statue you can cast in sand and decorate with a mosaic of pebbles and stones. And there are other ideas for decorating with **stone**, including painted rocks that make borders and accents for beds and a garden plaque painted on **slate**.

Terra cotta (**clay**) flower pots – those useful, inexpensive, widely available containers – are versatile surfaces for decorating that can assume a variety of guises. In this book, you'll find pots used as planters and as the base for windchimes. Pots also can be garden ornaments, birdbaths and feeders, fountains, tableware, and table bases.

You'll find painted **fabric** projects, too, including a doormat and pillows for patio furniture.

■ Brushes & Applicators

Artist's Paint Brushes

Artist's paint brushes – flats, rounds, and liners – are used for painting designs and for lettering. Experienced painters recommend you use the best brushes you can afford and clean and care for them meticulously so they will last. Two good guidelines for choosing brushes are to use the size brush that fits the design and feels comfortable to you.

Why Choose Waterbase Paints?

Because waterbase paints have so many advantages and are so readily available, they were used for all the projects in this book. Some advantages include:

- They have less odor because they contain far less solvent than oil-base paints, and so are much less apt to provoke headache or nausea. Some types are considered non-toxic.
- Cleanup is easy with soap and water, so the painter is not exposed to solvents in the cleaning of tools or brushes.
- They are safer to use indoors and not nearly as polluting as solvent based paints in their manufacturing process or in the volatile organic compounds (VOCs) they release after application.

Foam or Sponge Brushes

Foam brushes are handy for base painting and for applying crackle medium, decoupage finish, or glue.

Varnish Brushes

Varnish brushes are short-bristle brushes used for applying varnish. They come in a variety of widths.

Sponges

Sponges are useful for applying paint to create textures and designs. Compressed sponges, which you buy dry and flat, can be cut into shapes with scissors and hydrated to make sponge shapes for stamping.

■ Finishes

Aerosol Finishes

Aerosol finishes are clear-drying spray-on coatings that protect surfaces from moisture and dust. They are available in flat, satin, and gloss sheens. For best results, use several thin coats rather than one thick one. Be sure you purchase a finish that is recommend for outdoor use.

Brush-on Outdoor Sealers

Outdoor sealers are specifically designed for sealing and protecting surfaces that will be used outdoors. They are polyurethane based and clear-drying.

Preparing Surfaces

Wood

If you buy your piece already base painted, you need only make sure it's clean before painting your design on it.

Old Wood Preparation:

If you are painting an old wood piece, sand it well – first with medium grit, then fine grit sandpaper. Sand with the grain of the wood. Wipe away sanding dust with a tack cloth. If there are any holes, fill them with wood putty and let dry. Sand these areas smooth and wipe away dust. Then base paint the piece with the appropriate color.

Unfinished Wood Preparation:

New, unfinished wood pieces need to be sanded with fine sandpaper, sanding with the grain of the wood. Wipe away dust, then base paint with the appropriate color.

Metal

Primed or finished metal surfaces need only be dusted to be ready for painting. Galvanized tin pieces should be wiped with rubbing alcohol to remove the oily residue. Washing is not recommended because water can be trapped in seams and crevices, but if metal pieces are washed, be sure they are thoroughly dry before proceeding.

Clay Pots

1. Wash pots with vinegar and water to remove any dirt or oils. Scrub them with a brush if necessary. Let pots air dry completely.
2. If holes need to be drilled, use a carbide masonry drill bit. Make the holes *before painting*, in case the pot or saucer gets broken or develops a crack during drilling.
3. Paint the project according to the individual project instructions.
4. When paint is dry, apply the varnish of your choice to protect the painting.

SOME CAUTIONS:

• *Do not* paint the insides of pots if you plan to plant live plants directly in the pot. That said, we recommend you *not* plant directly in the pot. Clay pots are porous, and as water migrates from the inside of the pot to the outside, it will damage your painting. For best results, and to preserve your painting, place another pot inside your painted pot to hold plants.

• If you are determined to plant directly in your decorated pot, you can preserve the outside by sealing the inside with a waterbase sealer/finish; or use an outdoor sealer on both outside and inside of pot. Give it one or two good coats and allow to dry thoroughly.

• If using pots to present or store food, *do not* allow the food to come into contact with a painted surface. Use plastic liners, glass containers, or plastic bags to contain foods if the pot is painted on the inside. (It's okay for food to contact a clean, unpainted clay surface.)

Base Painting

The base paint is the foundation upon which you build your decorative effects – you can sponge over it, rag it, add decorative painted elements, distress it, crackle it, or antique it. Because it is your foundation, you want it to be smooth and to have thoroughly covered the surface. Apply base paint with a small roller or a wide fine-bristled brush. Apply one light coat and allow it to dry. Sand with fine sandpaper to smooth the surface. Apply a second coat and allow it to dry thoroughly. You are now ready to enjoy your piece or to add additional decorative effects.

Transferring Patterns

The patterns for the projects that require them are located on adjacent pages to the project. Follow this procedure to transfer a pattern:

1. Trace the pattern from the book onto tracing paper. Enlarge or reduce, if necessary, on a photocopier so the design fits your intended pot.
2. Position the traced pattern on your project. Slip transfer paper, shiny side down, between the project and the traced pattern.
3. Re-trace the pattern lines *lightly* with a stylus to transfer the design.

Painting a Design

Step-by-step painting instructions are provided for each project. Typically, the design elements are painted in solidly with the colors given. Shading and/or highlighting usually are added with washes or floats of color.

Painting Terms & Techniques

Base Painting: Covering a surface with paint before decorating with a painted design or other technique. Brush on the paint, using long, smooth strokes. Work carefully to avoid runs, drips, or sags.

Basecoat: The first layer of paint in a painted design.

Wash: A wash is an application of thinned paint that can be achieved in two ways. You can thin your paint to a wash consistency by adding **water** or a **floating medium** to the paint on your palette. Another way is to first fill your brush with floating medium. Dip a corner of the brush in the paint color, then stroke the brush back and forth on the palette to distribute and thin the paint in the brush. You can use washes of color to **shade** or **highlight** designs.

Outlining: Thin paint on palette with water or floating medium to achieve a consistency like that of ink. Pull a script liner through the paint, twisting the brush as you pull it out of the puddle to create a nice point on the brush. Outline design in smooth, long strokes. Reload brush as needed.

Stenciling

When a design element is repeated, it is sometimes easier to stencil that element rather than to paint it over and over. You can buy pre-cut stencils in a huge array of design motifs or you can cut a stencil yourself using a pattern from this book. Using a stencil is especially helpful when you want each of the elements to be exactly the same. For example, it is much easier to use a stencil for a checkerboard than try to paint it evenly each time.

Some projects in this book use simple stencils you can easily cut yourself. Patterns are provided for the designs. You can choose to cut the design as a stencil or simply transfer it to the surface and paint it.

To cut a stencil:
1. Place a piece of stencil blank material over the pattern. Trace the pattern on the stencil blank with a fine point permanent ink marker.
2. Place the stencil blank on a cutting surface such as glass (with edges covered with tape for safety) or a self-healing cutting mat. Cut along traced lines with a craft or utility knife or use an electric stencil cutting tool.
   - If using a knife, be sure your blade is very sharp and change blades as needed.
   - Keep the knife on the stencil for the full length of the cut to make a smooth line. Instead of moving the knife, move the stencil blank against the knife blade.

To stencil your design:
To stencil a design, use acrylic craft paint and a stencil brush.

Precautions & Tips

- Read product labels carefully and observe all manufacturer's recommendations and cautions.
- **Always** work in a well-ventilated area or outdoors. Avoid breathing fumes of paints and finishes.
- Wear gloves to protect your hands.
- Wear a dust mask or respirator to protect yourself from dust and fumes.
- Use a piece of old or scrap vinyl flooring for a work surface. Vinyl flooring is more protective and more convenient than layers of newspaper or plastic sheeting. Paint or finishes can seep through newspapers, and newspapers always get stuck to your shoes. Plastic sheeting is slippery. Spills can be wiped up quickly from vinyl, and nothing will seep through it to your floor. Small pieces of vinyl can be purchased inexpensively as remnants at floor covering stores and building supply centers.
- Dispose of solvents properly. If in doubt of how to dispose of them, contact your local government for instructions. Do not pour solvents or paint strippers down drains or toilets.

Photo 1: Cutting a checkerboard stencil.

Photo 2: Stenciling the design.

1. Position the stencil on the surface and tape in place.

2. Dip brush into paint on the palette. Dab brush on a paper towel to remove excess paint and to distribute paint evenly in the brush. *Tip:* You need very little paint on your brush – almost a dry brush. Excess paint on the brush will cause the color to run under the stencil.

3. *For even coverage,* apply paint to the cutout areas of the stencil in a circular motion. *For heavier coverage,* apply paint with a pouncing motion.

Cleaning up:

Clean the stencil by placing it on a stack of paper towels and wiping it with a damp cloth. Stubborn, dried paint can be removed with alcohol or brush cleaner.

Clean brushes with brush cleaner.

Applying Finishes

If you haven't used indoor/outdoor paint for your decorating, you will want to give your finished piece a protective coating. Varnishes and sealers are available in a variety of finishes – matte, satin, and gloss. Satin is my favorite. It gives a nice luster but doesn't emphasize uneven brush strokes like a gloss finish can.

Use waterbase varnishes and sealers that are compatible with acrylic paints for sealing and finishing. They are available in brush-on and spray formulations. Choose products that are non-yellowing and quick drying.

Apply the finish according to the manufacturer's instructions. Several thin coats are better than one thick coat. Let dry between coats according to the manufacturer's recommendations. A piece that will be used in the garden will need more coats of sealer or varnish for protection than a piece that will be used on a covered porch. ❏

Distressing

Charm can be added to your pieces by making them look like they have had loving use. This effect can be easily achieved by slightly sanding your finished painting with medium grit **sandpaper**. Sand in areas that would normally show use – corners, edges or areas near knobs, and handles. Remove a little of the paint so the underlying surface shows. Seal the project after distressing.

Antiquing

To make the piece look like the color has unevenly darkened with age, try antiquing. You can use a **pre-mixed antiquing medium** or mix your own with **acrylic paint** (Burnt Umber or Raw Umber or a color of your choice) and **glazing medium**. Test your mix to see if you like the intensity – you can add more paint or more glaze to achieve your desired effect.

Use a sponge brush, sponge roller, or an old rag to wipe antiquing over your painted design. Then wipe immediately with a clean cloth to remove the excess. For a deeper tone, reapply. Allow to dry thoroughly and varnish when dry.

This technique can be done on many projects in this book – even clay pots.

Photo 1: Mixing an antiquing glaze with glazing medium and acrylic paint.

Photo 2: Applying the antiquing glaze to the surface.

Combining Distressing and Antiquing

Distressing and antiquing can be combined for yet another effect. After distressing, antique the project using a brown mix (glazing medium + Burnt Umber). The brown color will stain the areas that were uncovered by sanding. Allow to dry, then varnish.

This technique can be done on many projects in this book – even clay pots.

Birdhouses in a Row Potting Bench

This charming potting bench was handmade from pine boards.
It is simply constructed and has a rustic appeal. The decorative painting
on the front of the bench gives the piece "show-off" status.

By Kathleen Taylor

SUPPLIES

Project Surface:
Wooden potting stand, hand made

Paints, Mediums & Finishes:
Acrylic craft paints
  Aqua
  Bright Pink
  Charcoal Grey
  French Blue
  Light Blue
  Lime Light
  Mint Green
  Mystic Green
  Poppy Red
  Portrait
  Sunflower
  True Blue
  Turquoise
  Wicker White
Indoor/outdoor gloss acrylic enamel - Vanilla
Outdoor sealer, satin

Tools & Other Supplies:
Foam brush for base painting
Various sizes of artist brushes including:
  1/2" flat, #8 round, #0 liner
Stencil brush, 1/2"
Masking tape, 1/2" wide

INSTRUCTIONS

Prepare:
1. Base paint stand with Vanilla indoor/outdoor gloss paint. Let dry. One light coat was painted on to give a stained effect rather than a solidly painted look.
2. Paint the sink part of the stand with a wash of Sunflower. Let dry. (Mix the paint with water to create a wash.)
3. Paint upper and lower rims of the sink part of the stand with a wash of French Blue.
4. Paint the crosspieces that support the sink paint with a wash of True Blue.
5. Transfer pattern to surface, using photo as a guide for placement.

Paint the Design:
Flowers
1. Mix Poppy Red with a little Wicker White to make a lighter color. Basecoat flowers with this mix.
2. Paint centers of flowers with Sunflower.
3. Paint inner flower shapes with a mix of equal parts Poppy Red and Wicker White.
4. Outline flower centers and paint the broken line border on flowers with Poppy Red.
5. Paint dots in centers with Poppy Red.
6. Paint the stitch pattern that outlines center flower area with Sunflower.

Leaves
1. Basecoat leaves and stems with Mystic Green.
2. Paint veins and outline leaves with Mint Green.

Birdhouses
Birdhouses are numbered from left to right.
1. Basecoat birdhouse #1 with Lime Light. Basecoat birdhouse #2 with Poppy Red. Basecoat birdhouse #3 with Turquoise. Let dry.
2. Outline roofs with masking tape. Lay a piece of tape vertically in the center of the birdhouse. Mark off 1/2" on each side and place another strip of tape on each side. Using a stencil brush, paint the stripes on birdhouse #1 with Sunflower, on birdhouse #2 with Portrait, and on birdhouse #3 with Mint Green. Remove tape.

Continued on page 16

Continued from page 14

3. Paint roofs and sides of all birdhouses with True Blue. Paint stripes on these areas with Light Blue.

4. Paint the entrance hole of each birdhouse with a mix of Charcoal Grey and a little Wicker White. Shade with Charcoal Grey.

5. Underline the roof on birdhouse #1 with Bright Pink, on birdhouse #2 with Aqua, and on birdhouse #3 with Poppy Red.

6. Paint the checked border around the circle on birdhouse #1 with Aqua, on birdhouse #2 with Poppy Red, and on birdhouse #3 with Bright Pink.

7. Paint the front door on birdhouse #1 with Bright Pink and outline the door with Poppy Red. Paint the door on birdhouse #2 with Aqua and outline the door with Turquoise. Paint the front door on birdhouse #3 with Poppy Red and outline the door with Poppy Red + a little Wicker White. Let dry.

Finish:
Varnish with outdoor sealer. ❏

Patterns
(actual size)

Patterns for Welcome to My Garden Sign
Instructions appear on page 18.
Enlarge pattern @200% for actual size.

Welcome to My Garden Sign

What a clever way to use a dust pan. The handle of the dust pan can be used for the hanger of this garden sign. Loop the handle over the picket of a fence to welcome visitors.

By Karen Embry

SUPPLIES

Project Surface:

Professional-size aluminum metal dust pan

Paints, Mediums & Finishes:

Acrylic craft paints

Azure Blue

Buckskin Brown

Dove Gray

Green Light

Lemonade

Licorice

Light Periwinkle

Olive Green

Red Violet

School Bus Yellow

Sky Blue

Van Dyke Brown

Wicker White

Yellow Citron

Outdoor sealer, satin

Brushes:

Wash - 1"

Script - 0, 2/0

Bright (flat) - #10

Angulars - 1/4", 1/2"

Old scruffy brush (for dry brushing), 1/2"

Old toothbrush (for spattering)

Tools & Other Supplies:

Rubbing alcohol

INSTRUCTIONS

Prepare:

1. Wipe dust pan with rubbing alcohol.
2. Apply one coat of outdoor sealer. Let dry.
3. Base paint the pan vertically with a streaky coat of a combination of Sky Blue, Azure Blue, and Red Violet. Let dry.
4. Transfer the design from page 17.

Paint the Design:

Leaves

1. Basecoat with Green Light.
2. Float bottom edges of leaves with Olive Green.
3. Dry brush centers of leaves with Yellow Citron.
4. Paint linework on leaves with Yellow Citron.

Flowers

1. Basecoat centers with Van Dyke Brown. Let dry.
2. Dry brush centers with Buckskin Brown.
3. Basecoat petals with School Bus Yellow.
4. Float edges of petals with Buckskin Brown.
5. Paint tiny dots near flower centers with Van Dyke Brown.

Bee

1. Basecoat body with School Bus Yellow. Float one side of body with Buckskin Brown.
2. Basecoat wings with Wicker White. Float edges of wings with Dove Gray.
3. Paint stripes on bee and antennae with Licorice.

Lettering

Paint with Licorice. Let dry.

Finish:

1. Spatter with Wicker White, using a toothbrush. Dip toothbrush in thinned "inky" white paint. Pull a craft stick or your thumb across the bristles, aiming the spray of paint at the project. Let dry.
2. Apply one coat of outdoor satin sealer. ❏

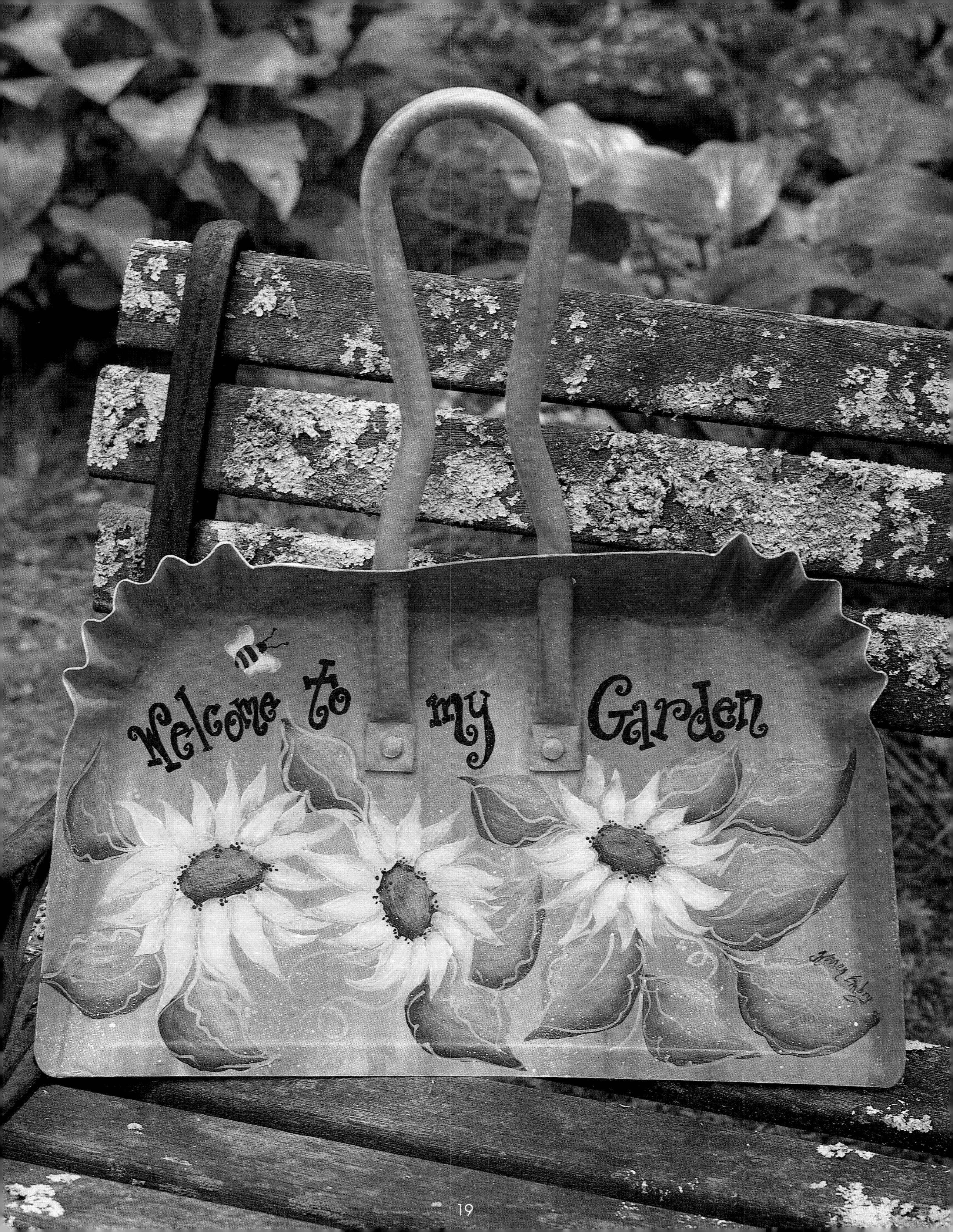
Welcome to my Garden

Plastic Pizzazz Chair & Table

Paints designed especially for painting on plastic make it easy to change the color or add designs to plastic furniture and accessories.

See the following pages for instructions.

Plastic Pizzazz Chair

By Kathy Ward

SUPPLIES

Project Surface:
White plastic patio chair

Paints & Sealers:
Paint for plastic
    Bright Yellow
    Cobalt
    Crimson
    Green
    Green Apple
    Light Blue
    Light Pink
    Purple
Paint for plastic sealer
Optional: Paint for plastic primer

Brushes & Painting Tools:
Flat sponge brushes, 1", 2", and 3"
1" square foam block
Round sponge-on-a-stick applicators,
    3/4" and 1/4" diameters
Craft tip set
Combing tool
#2 round brush
Stencil roller

Other Tools & Supplies:
Low-tack masking tape, 2" wide
Chisel point permanent black marker
Stencil blank material
Craft knife
Rubbing alcohol
Optional: Sandpaper

INSTRUCTIONS

Prepare:

1. Clean entire painting surface with alcohol. *If surface is shiny,* lightly sand *or* prime with two coats of paint for plastic primer.
2. Trace the patterns (wave and leaf) provided on stencil blank material. Cut out with a craft knife. Set aside.
3. Make a Cobalt glaze, mixing 1 part Cobalt paint with 3 parts sealer.

Paint the Design:

Arms & Seat Front

1. Tape off upper and lower edges of arms on chair. Using a 2" sponge brush, apply Cobalt glaze inside the taped off area. Immediately comb through the glaze with a curving motion, using the combing tool.
2. Tape off bottom front edge of chair. Using a 2" sponge brush, apply Cobalt glaze inside the taped off area. Immediately comb through the glaze with a curving motion, using the combing tool. Let dry.

Seat

1. Using a 2" sponge brush, paint Bright Yellow stripes on the chair seat. (Follow the 2" indentations on the chair *or,* if your chair is flat, tape off area with 2" tape.) Let dry.
2. Using a 1" sponge brush, paint Purple stripes across the seat. Let dry.
3. Using the angled edge of a 2" sponge brush, add narrow stripes with Green Apple going both ways for a plaid effect. *Tip:* Drag your pinky to steady your hand for a straight line. Let dry.
4. Paint cherries, using the 3/4" round sponge applicator with Crimson. Let dry.
5. About 2" above each pair of cherries, stencil pairs of Green leaves, using the 1" foam block. Let dry.
6. Highlight the leaves with Green Apple. Let dry.

Back

1. Paint the back slats of the chair with Light Blue, using a 1" sponge brush. Let dry.
2. Lay the chair down on its back. Paint center wavy line of the vine design on every other Light Blue slat, using the craft tip on the bottle of Green paint.
3. While the paint is still wet, use a #2 brush to pull out leaf-like 1/2" strokes on each side of the center vine.
4. Then using the #2 brush, highlight the leaves randomly with Green Apple. Let dry.
5. While chair is still on its back, position wave stencil along top edge of chair. Using the foam block, stencil the design with Light Pink.
6. Dot each end of the stenciled designs, using the 3/4" round sponge applicator. Let dry.

Legs

1. Stand up chair. Create the tassels on either side of the seat by applying a Light Pink dot with the 3/4" sponge applicator.
2. Dip the angled tip of the 3" sponge brush in Light Pink and apply feathery lines below the dots. Let dry.
3. Using the 1/4" sponge applicator, dot the four legs, inside the arms, and the back of the seat with Green Apple. Let Dry.

Outline

Use the photo as a guide.

1. Using the black marker, outline the edges of the pink wave designs.
2. Outline leaves and cherries and add stems.
3. Outline and add details on tassels.
4. With the chisel point of the marker, draw lines 1/2" apart around the chair back and the top edge of the chair.

Finish:

Using a stencil roller, apply sealer to entire chair. Let dry. ❏

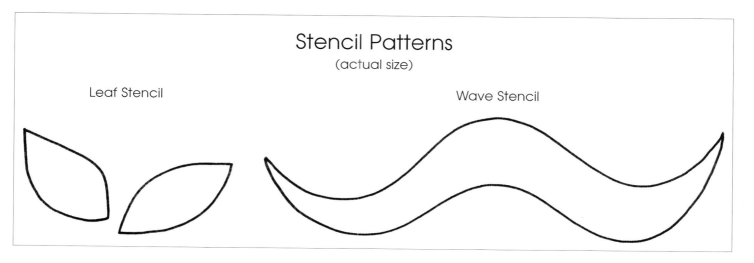

Stencil Patterns
(actual size)

Leaf Stencil

Wave Stencil

Plastic Pizzazz Table

By Kathy Ward

SUPPLIES

Project Surface:

White plastic side table

Paints & Finishes:

Paint for plastic

Cobalt

Green

Green Apple

Light Blue

Light Yellow

Purple

Paint for plastic sealer

Optional: Paint for plastic primer

Brushes & Painting Tools:

Flat sponge brushes, 1" and 2"

1" square foam block

Round sponge-on-a-stick applicators,
1-1/2", 5/8", and 1/4" diameters

Combing tool

Stencil roller

Other Tools & Supplies:

Chisel point black permanent marker

Stencil blank material

Craft knife

Rubbing alcohol

Optional: Sandpaper

INSTRUCTIONS

Prepare:

1. Clean entire painting surface with alcohol. *If surface is shiny,* lightly sand *or* prime with two coats of paint for plastic primer.
2. Trace the leaf pattern provided on page 23 onto stencil blank material. Cut out with a craft knife. Set aside.
3. Make a Cobalt glaze, mixing 1 part Cobalt paint with 3 parts sealer.

Paint the Design:

Top

1. With 2" sponge brush, paint every other slat with Light Blue.
2. Paint remaining slats with Purple. Let dry.
3. Dot flowers with Green Apple, using the 1-1/2" round sponge applicator. Let dry.
4. Dot flower centers using a 5/8" round sponge applicator with Light Yellow. Let dry.
5. Stencil leaves with Green, using the 1" foam square.
6. Dab sponge square in Green Apple and highlight. Let dry.

Legs

1. Brush Cobalt glaze cross pieces. Immediately comb through the glaze with a downward curving motion using the combing tool.
2. Using 1/4" round sponge applicator, apply dots to the legs with Green Apple.

Outline

1. Using the black permanent marker, loosely outline the leaves and flowers and dot the Light Blue slats of table.
2. Using the flat end of the chisel point of the marker, make stripes around edge of tabletop.

Finish:

Using a stencil roller, apply sealer to entire table. Let dry. ❏

Garden Angel Birdfeeder

By Patty Cox

SUPPLIES

Project Surface:
3/4" plywood, 23" x 16"

Paints & Finishes:
Indoor/outdoor gloss enamel paints
  Apricot
  Damask Blue
  Lilac
  Mojave Sunset
Acrylic craft paints
  Black
  Bright Blue
  Bright Green
  Orange
  Pale Green
  Pink
  Purple
  Raw Sienna
  Red Iron Oxide
  White
  Yellow Gold
Clear spray polyurethane finish

Other Tools & Supplies:
Artist paint brushes
Jigsaw
Sandpaper
2 spring tube benders, 5/8"
Metal rod, 3/8" x 28"
Metal rod, 3/8" x 12"
Drill and drill bits
Old high heel shoes
Polyurethane foam sealant
7" terra cotta saucer
Wood screw and washer
Compressed sponge

INSTRUCTIONS

Prepare:
1. Cut angel from plywood using a jigsaw.
2. Sand wood.
3. Drill holes in plywood edges for leg rods and terra cotta saucer.
4. Transfer pattern to wood.

Basecoat:
1. Paint dress with periwinkle (Lilac and Damask Blue).
2. Paint face with Apricot.
3. Paint hair with Mojave Sunset.

Continued on page 28

continued from page 26

Section A

Sponge:

1. Cut sponge shapes according to patterns.
2. Sponge squares on dress with Lilac. Let dry.
3. Sponge flowers with Orange.
4. Sponge spirals with Bright Blue and Purple.
5. Sponge flowers with Yellow Gold at an angle over orange flowers.
6. Sponge leaves with Bright Green around flowers.

Paint Face & Accessories:

1. Paint cheeks with a mix of Yellow Gold and Orange.
2. Paint lips with a mix of Orange and Pink.
3. Paint eye with Mojave Sunset. Paint pupil with Black.
4. Paint eyelid with periwinkle (Lilac and Damask Blue).
5. Outline face details with Mojave Sunset.
6. Paint shoes with periwinkle (Lilac and Damask Blue). Let dry.
7. Paint spring tube benders with Red Iron Oxide.
8. Sponge some areas of tube benders with Raw Sienna.

Finish:

Spray angel, shoes, and springs with polyurethane finish. Let dry.

Drill hole

Assemble:

1. Remove shoe lining and any metal supports from both shoes.
2. Drill a 3/8" hole in left shoe from inside the heel area of the show through the plastic heel. Drill a 3/8" hole in right shoe, about 3/4" into heel.
3. Glue the 12" rod in the drilled hole of the right shoe.
4. Slide the left shoe on the 28" metal rod. Glue shoe to rod with 12" of the rod above the heel of the shoe.
5. Stand shoes upright. Fill each shoe with polyurethane foam sealant. Let dry.
6. Cut away excess foam sealant from top of shoe with serrated knife.
7. Paint foam with gray (Black and White).
8. Slide spring tube benders on each rod. Glue rods in drilled holes of angel's body.
9. Attach terra cotta saucer to hand top with wood screw and washer. ❏

Sponge Pattern
(actual size)

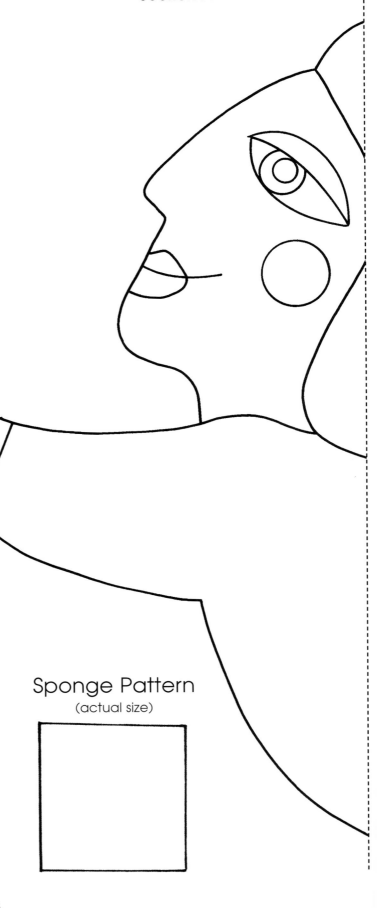

Pattern for Garden Angel

Connect Section A to Section B at dotted lines for complete pattern.

Enlarge pattern @180% for actual size.

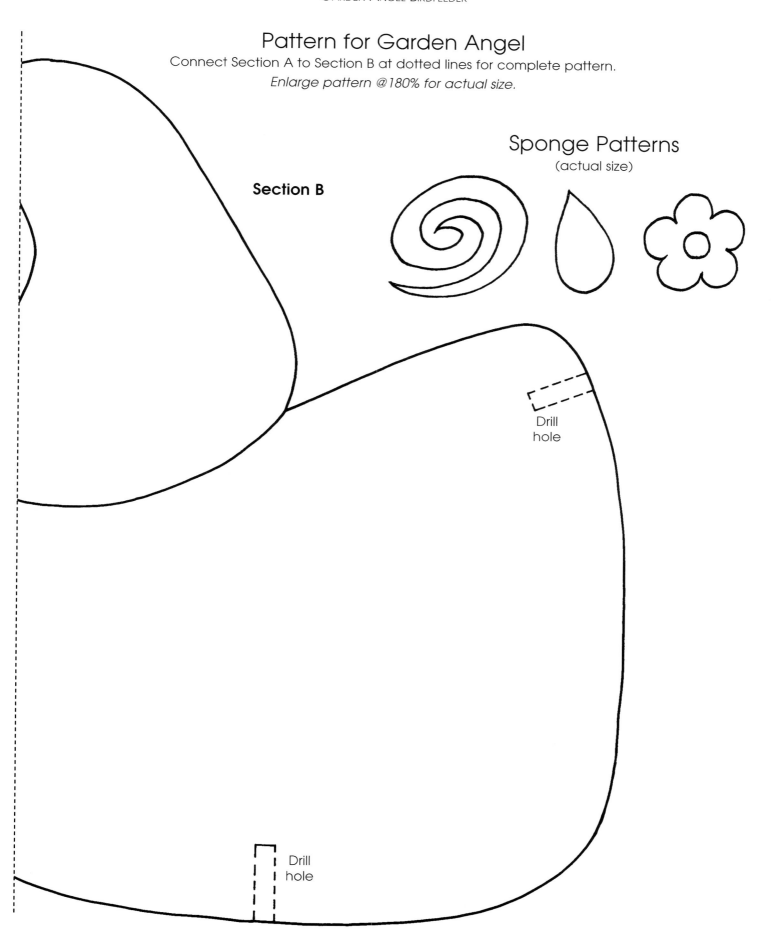

Section B

Sponge Patterns
(actual size)

Drill hole

Drill hole

Cheery Rooster Birdhouse

By Kathleen Taylor

SUPPLIES

Project Surface:
Wooden 3-story birdhouse

Paints & Finishes:
Acrylic craft paints
    Buckskin Brown
    Light Periwinkle
    Poppy Red
    Primrose
    Purple
    Solid Bronze (metallic)
    Tangerine
Artists' acrylic paints
    Naphthol Crimson
    Pure Black
    Pure Orange
    Raw Umber
    Turner's Yellow
    Yellow Ochre
Indoor/outdoor gloss acrylic enamel
    paints
    Ink Blue
Outdoor sealer, satin finish

Artist Brushes:
Flat - 1/2"
Liner - #0

Tools & Other Supplies:
Sponge brush for base painting
Copper carpet cut tacks, size #4
Medium grit sandpaper

INSTRUCTIONS

Prepare the surface:
1. Paint birdhouse with Ink Blue. Let dry.
2. Lightly sand for a rustic look. Wipe clean.
3. Paint roof with Turner's Yellow. Let dry.
4. Paint rim and underside of roof with Purple.
5. Transfer pattern to birdhouse.

Paint the Design:
Checks
Paint checks on each side of each corner of birdhouse with Light Periwinkle, using a 1/2" flat brush. Stagger checks on adjacent sides for a checkerboard effect.

Rooster
1. Basecoat body with Naphthol Crimson.
2. Paint broken line outline with Poppy Red using liner brush.
3. Paint star with metallic Solid Bronze.
4. Paint top half of beak with Turner's Yellow and bottom half with Yellow Ochre.
5. Paint eye with Pure Black using liner brush.
6. Basecoat comb with Pure Orange. Paint stripes on comb with Tangerine.
7. Basecoat legs and feet with Buckskin Brown. Paint stripes on legs and feet with Raw Umber. Let dry.

Finish:
1. Lightly sand the finished painting for an antique look.
2. Varnish with outdoor sealer. Let dry.
3. Hammer a copper tack at the point of each star. ❏

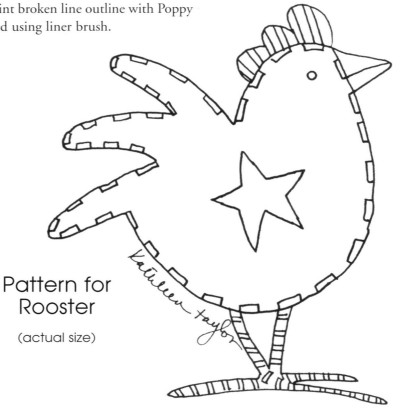

Pattern for Rooster

(actual size)

Insect Pots

By Kathleen Taylor

SUPPLIES

Painting Surface:
Three clay 4" rose pots and saucers

Paints & Finishes:
Acrylic craft paints
  Baby Pink
  Bright Pastel Green
  Buttercup
  Calico Red
  Cinnamon
  Coffee Bean
  Kelly Green
  Lavender
  Lemonade
  Light Blue
  Mystic Green
  Parchment
  Poppy Red
  Purple Lilac
  Sterling Blue
  Thunder Blue
  Violet Pansy
  Wicker White
Artists' acrylic paints
  Naphthol Crimson
  Pure Black
  Raw Umber
  Yellow Ochre
Outdoor sealer, satin finish

Brushes:
Stencil brush - 1/2"
Flat brush - 1/4"

Tools & Other Supplies:
Painter's masking tape, 1" wide
Medium grit sandpaper

INSTRUCTIONS

Prepare:
1. Seal the pots inside and out with outdoor sealer. Let dry.
2. Place six evenly spaced vertical strips of tape around the sides of each pot.
3. Paint the stripes between tape strips with these colors:
   Ladybug Pot - Sterling Blue
   Spider Pot - Buttercup
   Bumblebee Pot - Poppy Red
   Remove tape and let dry.
4. Transfer a different insect pattern to each pot.

Paint the Design:
LADYBUG POT
Ladybugs
1. Basecoat with Naphthol Crimson.
2. Paint details and outline bodies with Pure Black.

Details
1. Paint dots along each stripe with Light Blue.
2. Paint pot rim with Parchment. Let dry.
3. Paint stripes along top and bottom edges of pot rim with Thunder Blue, using a 1/4" flat brush.
4. Paint stripe on saucer rim with Thunder Blue. Let dry.
5. Lightly sand pot and saucer for a rustic look.

SPIDER POT
Spiders
1. Paint spiders' legs with Raw Umber.

2. Paint bodies with Coffee Bean.
3. Paint shadows with Raw Umber.
4. Paint dots on bodies with Cinnamon.

Details
1. Paint dots along each stripe with Lemonade.
2. Paint pot rim with Parchment. Let dry.
3. Paint stripes along top and bottom edges of pot rim with Calico Red, using a 1/4" flat brush.
4. Paint stripe on saucer rim with Calico Red. Let dry.
5. Lightly sand pot and saucer for a rustic look.

BUMBLEBEE POT
Bumblebee
1. Paint wings with Wicker White.
2. Paint bees' bodies and details with Pure Black.
3. Paint stripes on bodies with Yellow Ochre.

Details
1. Paint dots along each stripe with Baby Pink.
2. Paint pot rim with Parchment. Let dry.
3. Paint stripes along top and bottom edges of pot rim with Calico Red, using a 1/4" flat brush.
4. Paint stripe on saucer rim with Calico Red. Let dry.
5. Lightly sand pot and saucer for a rustic look.

Finish:
Varnish with outdoor sealer. ❑

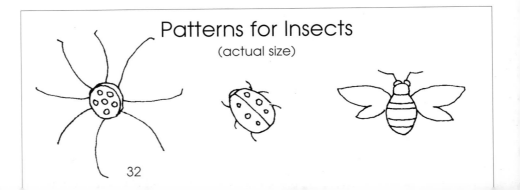

Patterns for Insects
(actual size)

Faux Majolica Plate

Majolica is a distinctive type of earthenware that is glazed with an enamel
tin-glaze process. In the Victorian era, leaves, shells, and other natural
motifs were all the rage on majolica plates, platters, and jugs.
This faux majolica technique uses fresh leaves from the garden and polymer clay to
reproduce this fashionable look with ease. Select a large broad leaf with good vein
detail such as grape, ivy, magnolia, or maple. *Note: The rolling pin and pasta machine
cannot be used with food after they have been used with the polymer clay. Do
not allow food to come in contact with plate. Use for decorative purposes or place
a clear plate on top or a napkin on the plate if you wish to use it as a serving piece.*

By Marie Browning

SUPPLIES

Project Surface:

Polymer clay - green

Fresh leaves

Glass plate - 10" diameter

Paints & Finishes:

Acrylic craft paints

   Green Olive

   Nutmeg

   Plum Chiffon

   Yellow Ochre

Two-part pour-on resin coating

Matte sealer spray

Paint Brushes:

Round - #4

Flat - 1/2"

Tools & Other Supplies:

Plastic mixing cups

Wooden stir stick

Glue brush

Paper cups

Wax paper

White glue

Pasta machine *or* wooden rolling pin

Craft knife

INSTRUCTIONS

Make the Leaves:

1. Condition the polymer clay until soft and pliable.
2. Run the clay through the pasta machine on the thickest setting to produce large, smooth flat sheets. *Option:* Roll out the clay with a wooden rolling pin to a 1/8" thickness.
3. Press fresh leaves into the clay by rolling the leaves and the clay through the pasta machine. *Tip:* Experiment – try the top of the leaf against the clay and the bottom of the leaf against the clay. Choose the method that gives you the best impression of the leaf with lots of vein detail.
4. Carefully remove the fresh leaf from the clay. With the craft knife, cut out the clay leaf shapes.
5. Carefully turn over the clay leaf. Brush on a thin coating of white glue.
6. Place the cut leaves on the plate, starting around the rim and working toward the center, pressing the leaves gently to the plate. Let set for about an hour while the white glue dries.
7. Carefully smooth all the cut edges with your finger so the leaves have a natural, "un-cut" look.

Bake:

Bake the plate with the polymer leaves in the oven, following the manufacturer's instructions. Let cool completely.

Paint the Clay Leaves:

Thin acrylic paints with water to make light washes of color. Add as many washes of color as you like to achieve the desired look. Use the photo as a guide.

1. Brush with thinned Green Olive.
2. Shade with thinned Purple Chiffon.
3. Wash thinned Nutmeg over the impressed vein details.

Continued on page 36

Faux Majolica Plate
continued from page 34

4. Add thinned Yellow Ochre to the edges of the leaves. Let dry completely.

Finish:

1. Cover your work surface with wax paper. Place the plate on paper cups to lift it off the work surface.

2. Mix 3 oz. pour-on resin according to the manufacturer's instructions and pour on the plate. Use the glue brush to spread the resin coating. Make sure the entire surface is covered. Remove any bubbles by gently exhaling on the plate. Let the plate sit undisturbed for 24 hours to set up. Dispose of the mixing cup, stir stick and glue brush – they can be used only once.

3. *Option:* Spray the plate with matte sealer finish for a matte look. ❑

Faux Mosaic Tray

With just a square of sponge and some paint, a plain surface can be made to look like an expensive mosaic. The treatment is so easy and such fun to do – it gives an updated, popular mosaic look without the expense, mess, weight, or bulk of ceramic tile.

This design is great for today's retro look – reminiscent of the pop art of the 1960s.

See instructions on the following pages.

Pictured on page 36-37

SUPPLIES

Project Surface:
Wooden serving tray, 11" x 15"

Paints & Finishes:
Acrylic craft paints (2 oz. bottles)
Black
Clay Bisque
Cobalt
White
Yellow Light
Gloss acrylic sealer, spray or brush-on

Tools & Other Supplies:
Sandpaper, medium and fine grades
Cellulose kitchen sponges
Pencil
Disposable palette
Sponge brush (for base painting)
Plain brown paper bag
Optional: Tracing paper, transfer paper

INSTRUCTIONS

Prepare & Base Paint:
1. Sand wood until smooth, starting with medium grade sandpaper and finishing with fine sandpaper. Wipe away dust.
2. Paint tray with several coats of Clay Bisque. (This paint is the color of sandy grout, and forms the background of the mosaic.) Allow to dry between coats. Sand between each coat with fine sandpaper and wipe away dust. After painting the final coat, allow to dry and rub the surface with pieces of a brown paper bag to smooth.
3. Using a pencil, sketch a rounded petal, daisy-like flower on the tray surface or transfer flower pattern from page 39 to surface of tray.

Sponge:
1. Cut dry cellulose sponges into 1/2" squares – one for each paint color you are using. Cut three more 1/2" squares and cut each into two triangles. Save remaining pieces of sponge – they can be used later to cut into smaller pieces to fill gaps.
2. Dampen all sponge pieces.
3. Begin with the blue border. Pour a puddle of blue paint on the palette. Dip a sponge square into the puddle, filling the sponge with paint. Lightly press sponge on a clean area of the palette to distribute paint evenly in sponge. Press sponge square in the four corners of the tray, using a stamping motion. Sponge a blue border around the edge of the tray, reloading sponge as needed. Allow a 1/8" to 1/16" space between each square as you stamp, and try to keep the same amount of space between each square. Rinse sponge when finished.

Making Faux Mosaic with Sponges

Photo 1: Cut sponge into squares to create stamps.

Photo 2. Dip sponge square into paint and stamp the squares onto surface.

4. Using a new square sponge, fill in the space around the flower outline with stamped white squares, working from the outside in. Use a triangle sponge as needed to fill areas around the flower.

5. Fill in the petals of the flower with yellow paint squares. Use triangles where needed to complete design. Use smaller pieces of sponge to fill in any gaps.

6. Fill in the center of the flower with black paint squares, using triangles where needed. Allow to dry for 24 or more hours.

Finish:
Apply gloss finish to tray. Allow to dry 48 hours before using. ❏

Pattern for Flower
(actual size)

Geranium Pots & Watering Can

By Rachel Wright

These garden pieces are decorated with flowering geraniums. The complementary colors make a coordinated garden display. The bucket and watering can I used came with a faux weathered patina finish. If you can't locate these, use a patina paint kit to create the finish on a galvanized tin watering can and bucket.

SUPPLIES

Project Surfaces:

Clay pot, 7"

Tall metal bucket with faux patina finish

Metal watering can with faux patina finish

Paints, Mediums & Finishes:

Acrylic craft paints

Medium Orange

Naphthol Crimson

School Bus Yellow

Tapioca

Thicket

True Burgundy

Floating medium

Outdoor spray varnish

Clay pot sealer

Brushes:

Flats - #16, #12

Liner - #5/0

Filbert - #6

Round - #1

Tools & Other Supplies:

Sea sponge

Palette paper

White transfer paper

Damp cloth

INSTRUCTIONS

Prepare & Base Paint:

1. Wipe dust from metal surfaces, using a damp cloth.
2. In a well-ventilated area, spray clay pot sealer on the outside and inside of the clay pot.
3. Load a damp (but not wet) sea sponge with Naphthol Crimson and Medium Orange. Pounce the colors over the top rim of the clay pot. Allow to dry.
4. Load a #1 round brush with Naphthol Crimson. Dip the tip in Medium Orange. Paint the stripes around the tops and bottoms of the bucket and watering can.
5. Transfer the pattern. *Option:* Paint the design freehand.

Painting the Design:

Larger Leaves

Use a #16 brush on the bucket and the watering can and a #12 on the pot.

1. Wet a flat brush and blot off excess water. Double load the brush with Thicket on one corner and Tapioca on the other. Blend the colors into the bristles by moving the brush back and forth on your palette. *Tip:* You will need a lot of paint loaded on the brush, and will need to dip into paint at least one or two more times.
2. Starting at the top of the larger round leaves, with the green side of the brush to the outside, paint the leaf. Start on the chisel edge, then push the bristles flat and wiggle the bristles, pivoting off of the center of the leaf back and forth. Wiggle all the way around the leaf. Re-load the brush as needed.
3. Load the flat brush with True Burgundy on one corner and floating medium on the other. Blend on palette. With the burgundy color to the outside edge, add a red tint on the inside of each wiggle leaf, pivoting around the centers.
4. Using the same methods above, switch to the #12 flat brush, and paint the leaves on the clay pots.

Smaller Leaves & Stems

1. Using a #12 flat brush double loaded with Thicket and Tapioca, paint the smaller leaves. Start on the chisel edge of the bristles, then push them flat, turn the bristles to the right or left (depending on the leaf), then lift back to the chisel edge.
2. Paint the stems using the 5/0 liner brush loaded with an inky Thicket (half paint, half water).

Geraniums

Each flower has four overlapping petals with rounded outside edges. Allow both the background flowers and foreground flowers to show in the finished design. It is not necessary to complete each flower. Since they grow in clusters, it is fine to have overlapping and partial petals throughout the design.

1. Wet the bristles of the #6 filbert brush and blot dry. Load fully with True Burgundy. Working from the outside of each small flower, stand the brush on the chisel edge of the bristles, then push and pull each petal into the center of the flower. (These are the background flowers.)
2. Load the #6 filbert with Naphthol Crimson. Dip the tips of the bristles in Medium Orange. Paint the foreground petals, overlapping some of the burgundy petals, allowing some of the background flowers to show through. *Tip:* Pick up more paint every couple of petals.
3. Using brush handle dipped in School Bus Yellow, dot the centers of the four-petal flowers.

Tendrils

Mix equal amounts Thicket and Tapioca. Dilute with water to make an inky consistency. Using the #5/0 liner brush loaded with this mixture, paint the curly tendrils, working on the tips of the bristles. Let dry.

Finish:

Spray each piece with outdoor sealer, working in a well-ventilated area or outdoors. Spray several light coats, allowing each to dry before adding the next. ❑

Pattern for Geranium Bucket, Pot & Watering Can

Enlarge patterns @ 135% for actual size.

Instructions appear on page 41.

Bucket

RACHEL

Clay Pot

RACHEL

Watering Can

RACHEL

Pattern for
Potting Shed
Sign

*Enlarge pattern
@ 210% for actual size.*
Instructions appear
on page 45.

POTTING SHED

Potting Shed Sign

This sign sports a crackled finish and copper wire trim. Copper wire also forms a loop for holding a terra cotta pot. The copper wire trim at top of plaque can be fashioned as shown here, or as shown on diagram on page 43 or photo on page 45.

By Patty Cox

SUPPLIES

Project Surface:

Plywood, 3/4" thick, 21" x 10-1/2"

Paints, Mediums & Finishes:

Indoor/outdoor gloss acrylic enamel paints

Fairway Green

Green Mint

Acrylic craft paint

Pine Green

Raw Sienna

Sand

Crackle medium

Spray polyurethane finish

Tools & Other Supplies:

Artist paint brushes

4 drawer pulls and screws, 1-1/4" to use as hangers

14" of 14 gauge copper wire (to hold terra cotta pot)

5 ft. 10 gauge copper wire for trim at top

28 gauge copper wire for wrapping copper trim

Industrial strength glue or cement

Terra cotta pot, 2-1/4"

Staple gun

Needlenose pliers

Sawtooth picture hanger

Drill and drill bits

INSTRUCTIONS

Paint & Crackle:

1. Paint front and sides of plywood with Fairway Green. Let dry.
2. Apply crackle medium to surface according to manufacturer's instructions. Let dry.
3. Paint sign Green Mint, using long strokes. Allow paint to dry and crackle.
4. Transfer lettering and vine patterns.

Paint the Design:

1. Paint letters with Sand. Let dry.
2. Float a Raw Sienna wash along edges of letters.
3. Double load brush with Pine Green and Sand. Paint vines.
4. Paint leaves with Pine Green.

Finish:

1. Drill four holes for drawer pulls to use for hanging items at sign bottom. Drill a hole for terra cotta pot wire placement. See indication of this area on pattern.
2. Screw drawer pulls in position.
3. Wrap the piece of 14" wire around the terra cotta pot. Twist wires 3/4" behind pot.
4. Insert wire ends and twisted section through center hole on sign. Open wire ends and staple to board back.
5. Cut two 18" lengths of 10 gauge copper wire or old hanger wire.
6. Grip wire end with needlenose pliers. Bend into s-scroll shape according to pattern. Repeat for other s-scroll. Connect scrolls with a wrap of 28 gauge wire.
7. Cut three 5" lengths of 10 gauge copper wire. Bend two into coil shapes and leave one straight.
8. Drill three holes in sign top. (See Pattern for indication of where holes are to be drilled.) Insert and glue straight wire in top center hole. Insert and glue a coiled wire piece in each top side hole.
9. Connect the s-scroll wire pieces to the two coil shapes glued in the top of the sign with wraps of 28 gauge wire.
10. Screw sawtooth picture hanger to top back of sign. ❑

Pictured at right: The sign with wire as decorative element.

Weed Garden Plaque

A quote from Ralph Waldo Emerson embellishes a painted plaque made from a wooden tray. Crackling and spattering give the plaque an antique look.

By Patty Cox

SUPPLIES

Project Surface:

Basswood tray or plaque, 9" x 12"

Paints, Mediums & Finishes:

Acrylic craft paints

Charcoal

Dark Olive Green

Light Olive Green

Off White

Indoor/outdoor gloss acrylic enamel paint

Barn Red

Chamois

Cumin

Crackle medium

Clear acrylic spray sealer

Tools & Other Supplies:

Artist paint brushes

Fine tip permanent black marker

Old toothbrush

Sandpaper

Drill and small drill bit

Sash lock hardware for lock and wood screws

Sawtooth picture hanger

Optional: Compressed sponge, craft knife

INSTRUCTIONS

Paint & Crackle:

1. Paint entire tray with a mix of Barn Red and Cumin. Let dry.
2. Apply crackle medium according to manufacturer's instructions. Let dry.
3. Brush Chamois over entire tray. Allow paint to dry and crackle.
4. Sand entire surface of tray with sandpaper. Wipe away dust.
5. Transfer lettering.

Paint the Design:

1. Paint lettering with Dark Olive Green.
2. Paint triangles with Barn Red. Let dry. *Option:* Cut a triangle-shaped piece of sponge and sponge triangles with Barn Red. Let dry.

continued on page 48

a weed
is a plant
whose virtues
have not been
discovered.
Emerson

continued from page 46

3. Sand surface, removing paint from lettering and triangles.
4. Outline lettering with fine tip black marker.
5. Paint greenery design around tray border with Dark Olive Green and Light Olive Green.
6. Use the handle end of a paintbrush to make dots around greenery, using the photo as a guide for color placement. Let dry.

Finish:

1. Spatter the tray with Charcoal, using an old toothbrush. Let dry.
2. Spray tray with clear sealer. Let dry.
3. Position sash lock at center bottom of tray.
4. Mark and drill pilot holes. Attach sash lock hook with wood screws.
5. Position picture hanger on top center back of tray.
6. Mark and drill pilot holes. Attach hanger with small nails.
❏

Pattern for Quote
(actual size)

a weed is a plant whose virtues have not been discovered.

Emerson

Pattern for Tray Rim

(actual size)

Reverse and repeat for opposite side.

Garden Helper

By Patty Cox

SUPPLIES

Project Surfaces:

Plywood, 3/4" thick, 15" x 25-1/2"

2 dowel sticks, 36" x 5/8" (for legs)

2 rusted hinges, 12" long (for arms)

Pair of old high-heel shoes

6" bucket with rusty finish

Small (child-size) rake

Paints & Finishes:

Indoor/outdoor gloss acrylic enamel
   paints

   Apricot

   Barn Red

   Damask Blue

   Green Mint

   Mojave Sunset

   Rose

   White

Rust spray paint

Acrylic craft paint - Raw Sienna

Clear polyurethane spray finish

Tools & Other Supplies:

Artist paint brushes

Jigsaw

Sandpaper

10 gauge copper wire *or* hanger wire

1" dowel (to curl wire hair)

Industrial strength glue

Round screw eyes, 1/2"

Four 1/2" two-hole straps and wood
   screws

Sponge

Portland cement

2 bricks

Optional: 2 strips of plastic foam,
   1/2" x 2" (such as Styrofoam®)

INSTRUCTIONS

Cut Out & Paint the Body:

1. Cut head and body from plywood, using a jigsaw. Sand wood.
2. Transfer pattern to wood.
3. Thin paints with water so the wood grain will show through the paint.
4. Paint the dress with Green Mint. Paint the apron with White.
5. Paint the face with Apricot, the cheeks with Rose, the lips with a mix of Rose and Barn Red, and the eyes with Blue Damask.
6. Outline everything with rust (Barn Red and Mojave Sunset). Let dry.
7. Spray painted figure with clear polyurethane finish. Let dry.
8. Install screw eyes at shoulders.

Add the Hair:

1. Wrap 10 gauge copper wire around a 1" dowel.
2. Drill two 1/8" holes at an angle on each side of head.
3. Add cement to one end of each piece of coiled wire. Insert a wire end in each hole.

Add Legs & Feet:

1. Remove heels from shoes. Punch a 1/2" diameter hole through each shoe at heel.
2. Paint the dowels with a wash of White paint. Let dry.
3. Spray dowels with polyurethane finish. Let dry.
4. Insert dowels through shoes at heel so the dowels take the place of the heels.
5. Push dowels into garden soil. Prop up with bricks as shown in photo. Mix cement. Pour cement into each shoe. Allow cement to set.
6. Paint the shoes and the "heels" with Damask Blue. Let dry.
7. Attach dowels to the back of the angel's skirt with hole straps.

Option: Wrap a foam strip around each dowel at the hole strap to secure.

Add Arms & Accessories:

1. Open screw eyes at shoulders. Hang a hinge on each screw eye.
2. Use wire to attach rake to one arm.
3. Attach the bucket to the other arm, using photo as a guide. ❏

Shoes supported while drying.

Pattern for Garden Helper
Enlarge pattern @200% for actual size.

Section A

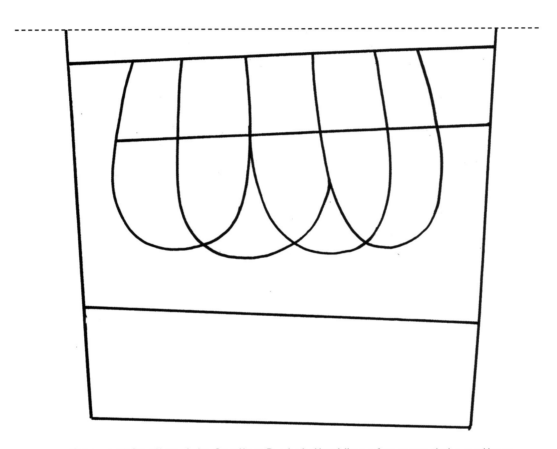

Connect Section A to Section B at dotted lines for complete pattern.

Section B

Picnic Serving Tub or Planter

How does your garden grow? "With love!" proclaims this tub. Use it on your porch, deck, or patio for serving snacks or drinks or to hold potted plants.

By Karen Embry

SUPPLIES

Project Surface:

Galvanized metal oblong tub, 5.5 gallon

Paints & Finishes:

Acrylic craft paints

Baby Pink

Buckskin Brown

Green Light

Lemonade

Licorice

Magenta

Olive Green

Pink

Purple Lilac

Red Violet

School Bus Yellow

Wicker White

Outdoor sealer, satin

Artist Brushes:

Wash - 1"

Script Liners - 0, 2/0

Angulars - 1/2"

Filberts - #6

Other Supplies:

Rubbing alcohol

INSTRUCTIONS

Prepare & Base Paint:

1. Wipe the tub with rubbing alcohol.
2. Apply one coat of outdoor sealer. Let dry.
3. Base paint with two coats of Lemonade. Let dry.
4. Transfer pattern.

Paint the Design:

1. Basecoat rosebuds with Baby Pink. Float bottoms of rosebuds with Magenta. Paint swirls with Magenta.
2. Basecoat half of each leaf with Green Light. Basecoat other half with Olive Green.
3. Paint stems and vines with Olive Green.
4. Over the Olive Green stems and vines, paint a thin line of Green Light.
5. Paint tiny dot trios around leaves with Olive Green.
6. Paint hearts with Purple Lilac. Float bottom side of each heart with Red Violet.
7. Basecoat Daisy Petals with Wicker White.
8. Paint centers of daisies with a blotchy pattern of School Bus Yellow and Buckskin Brown.
9. Paint lettering with Licorice. Let dry.

Finish:

Seal with two coats of outdoor satin sealer. ❏

Pattern

Enlarge pattern @150% for actual size.

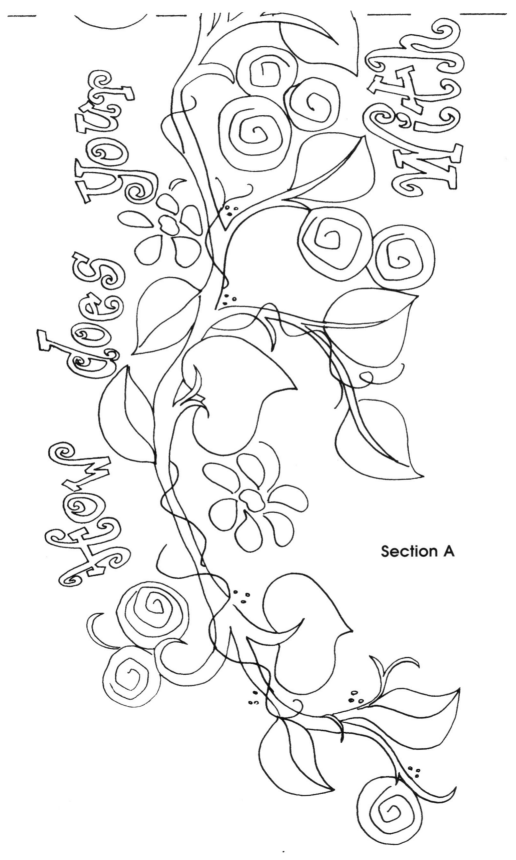

Section A

Connect Section A to Section B at dotted lines for complete pattern.

Section B

Rainbow Watering Can

By Karen Embry

SUPPLIES

Project Surface:

Metal watering can with pressed diamond design

Paints & Finishes:

Acrylic craft paints

Antique Gold (metallic)

Azure Blue

Inca Gold (metallic)

Magenta

Red Violet

School Bus Yellow

Titanium White

Outdoor sealer, satin

Artist Paint Brushes:

Bright (flat) - #10

Wash - 1"

Script liner - #0

Other Supplies:

Rubbing alcohol

INSTRUCTIONS

Prepare & Base Paint:

1. Wipe watering can with rubbing alcohol.
2. Basecoat entire watering can with Orchid. Let dry completely.
3. Apply Azure Blue, Red Violet, School Bus Yellow and Magenta randomly over the entire surface. While all colors are still wet, wipe them with a dry paper towel, leaving some color but also allowing some of the background color to show through. Let dry.
4. *Option:* Repeat step 3 if you prefer more intense color. Let dry.

Paint the Design:

1. Paint small bands going around watering can and area between can and handle with a mix of equal amounts of Antique Gold and Inca Gold.
2. Paint daisies, swirls, and lettering with Titanium White.
3. Paint daisy centers with School Bus Yellow.

Finish:

Apply two coats of outdoor satin sealer. ❑

Patterns
(actual size)

Handle   Rim   Sides

Floral Box Planter

By Karen Embry

SUPPLIES

Project Surface:

Wooden rectangular planter box

4 wooden balls or knobs with one flat side, 1-1/2" (for feet)

Paints, Mediums & Finishes:

Acrylic craft paints

Bright Baby Pink

Fresh Foliage

Gray Green

Hot Pink

Lemon Custard

Lime Yellow

Maple Syrup

Olive Green

Red Violet

Yellow Ochre

Blending medium

Outdoor sealer, satin

Artist Brushes:

Wash - 1"

Angular - 1/2"

Script liners - 0, 2/0

Other Supplies:

400 grit sandpaper

Wood glue

INSTRUCTIONS

Prepare, Seal & Base Paint:

1. Sand wooden box. Wipe away dust.
2. Mix equal amounts Gray Green paint and outdoor sealer. Paint box with this mixture. Let dry.
3. Paint box with Gray Green. Let dry.
4. Transfer the design.

Paint the Design:

Flowers

1. Basecoat petals with Bright Baby Pink. Let dry.
2. Float inside edges of petals (near stamen) with Hot Pink, walking the float about two-thirds of the way out on each petal. Let dry.
3. Again at the centers of petals, float over the previous float with Red Violet, bringing the float about one-third of the way out on the petals.
4. Paint lines on petals Red Violet.
5. Paint stamen with Maple Syrup. Highlight stamen with Yellow Ochre.
6. Paint some dots at the ends of stamen with Maple Syrup. Add some dots with Yellow Ochre. To highlight, paint a few dots with Lemon Custard.

Leaves & Vines

1. Basecoat leaves and vines with Olive Green.
2. Float the top sides of leaves with Fresh Foliage.
3. Paint veins on leaves with Lime Yellow.
4. Paint highlights on vines with Lime Yellow.

continued on page 62

continued from page 60

Finish:

1. Glue balls to the bottom of the box, one at each corner.
2. Apply one coat of outdoor satin sealer. ❑

Feet

1. Paint the wooden balls with Hot Pink. Let dry.
2. Add Lime Yellow dots to all of the balls. Let dry.

Section A

Pattern for Planter Box
(actual size)

Section B

Connect Section A to Section B at dotted lines for complete pattern.

SUPPLIES

Project Surfaces:

Wooden plaque

2 tin wall pockets

Paints & Finishes:

Acrylic craft paints

Azure Blue

Buttercream

Buttercup

Green Light

Lavender

Light Blue

Light Periwinkle

Lime Light

Magenta

Mint Green

Orange Light

Orchid

Patina

Pure Black

Pure Orange

Purple

Raw Sienna

Wicker White

Yellow Light

Outdoor sealer, satin

Artist Paint Brushes:

Wash Series - 1"

Flat - 1/2"

Bright (flat) - #10

Angulars - 1/4", 1/2"

Script liners - 0, 2/0

Other Supplies:

2 ft. thin rope or twine

4 screw eyes, 3/8"

Rubbing alcohol

400 grit sandpaper

Garden Sign with Plant Pockets

By Karen Embry

INSTRUCTIONS

Prepare, Seal & Base Paint:

1. Sand wooden plaque. Wipe away dust.
2. Mix equal amounts Buttercream paint and outdoor sealer. Paint plaque with this mixture. Let dry.
3. Paint the plaque with Buttercream. Let dry.
4. Wipe tin pockets with rubbing alcohol.
5. Transfer the design to the plaque.

Paint the Design:

Tin Pockets

1. Paint one stripe on one tin pocket with Lavender. Paint the other stripe with Orchid.
2. Paint one stripe on the other tin pocket with Orange Light. Paint the other stripe with Yellow Light.
3. Float bottom of Lavender stripe with Purple.
4. Float bottom of Orchid stripe with Magenta.
5. Float bottom of Orange Light stripe with Pure Orange.
6. Float bottom of Yellow Light stripe with Raw Sienna.

Bird

1. Basecoat bird with Patina.
2. Float bottom edge of bird's body and wings with Azure Blue. Let dry.
3. Dry brush Mint Green on wings and body.
4. Paint beak with Yellow Light. Float bottom with Raw Sienna.
5. Paint the eye with White. Paint pupil with Pure Black.

Clouds

1. Basecoat cloud in back with Wicker White. Float edge with Light Blue.
2. Basecoat cloud in front with Light Blue. Float bottom edge with Light Periwinkle. Float top with Wicker White.

Sun

Basecoat with Yellow Light. Let dry. Float edges with Raw Sienna.

Leaves

1. Basecoat leaves with Lime Light. Float one side of each leaf with Green Light.
2. Paint veins, swirls, and groups of three dots with Green Light.

Continued on page 66

continued from page 64

Flowers

See the numbers on the pattern.

1. Basecoat flowers #1 and #2 with Buttercup. Let dry. Float outer edges of the petals with Raw Sienna. Paint lines in petals with Raw Sienna.
2. Basecoat flowers #3 and #4 with Orange Light. Float outer edges of petals with Pure Orange. Paint lines in petals with Pure Orange.
3. Basecoat flowers #5 and #6 with Lavender. Float outer edges with Purple. Paint lines in petals with Purple.
4. Basecoat flowers #7 and #8 with Orchid. Float outer edges with Magenta. Paint lines in petals with Magenta.
5. Dry brush a little Yellow Light in the centers of all flowers.
6. Paint tiny dots in centers of flowers with Wicker White.

Lettering

1. Paint letters with Purple.
2. Highlight with Lavender. Let dry.

Finish:

1. Apply one coat of outdoor sealer to plaque and tin pockets. Let dry.
2. Attach two screw eyes on top of plaque. Thread twine through screw eyes to make a hanger.
3. Attach two screw eyes in front of plaque to hang tin pockets. See pattern for placement. Place tin pockets over screw eyes.

Section A

Patterns for Garden Sign
(actual size)

Section B

Connect Section A to
Section B at dotted lines for
complete pattern.

Birdhouse Row Fence

Sometimes a garden has to be located where the sun is – in this wooded suburban neighborhood, the best place for a vegetable and flower garden in this yard was right on the street. The picket fence, built of scrap lumber, provides a barrier and a border that defines the garden and discourages pedestrian and pet traffic.

Here and there, the fence's pickets are topped with little painted "roofs" that give the look of a birdhouse village. On the larger-dimension lumber used for the supporting posts, holes drilled partly through the posts resemble the entrance holes on birdhouses. Dowels inserted in drilled holes create perches for feathered friends.

The "roofs" and "birdhouses" on the posts were painted in a variety of lively colors. Indoor/outdoor gloss enamel paints will keep their fresh-painted look; for a distressed or aged appearance, use acrylic craft paints (which will fade and weather naturally outdoors over time if not protected with a sealer) or get an instantly aged look by sanding or crackling, then sealing.

There are numerous books that provide more detailed instructions for fence-building; it's also possible to buy sections of picket fence at home improvement stores and decorate them with this birdhouse theme.

Built by Ben Bishop

SUPPLIES

Lumber for posts, rails, pickets, and "roofs"

Dowels, 1/4" *or* 1/2"

Concrete or cement mix for setting posts

Galvanized screws and/or nails

Paints for "roofs" (see above)

Wood glue

Tools:

Post hole digger

Saw (a power miter saw makes it easy to cut angles for roofs and picket ends)

Drill with hole saw attachment, wood bits, and screw bit (if using screws)

Paint brushes

INSTRUCTIONS

1. Determine the size of your fence and where supporting posts should be placed.
2. Dig holes for posts with post hole digger. Insert poles and set in concrete. Let dry until set.
3. Build sections of rails and pickets and attach to posts.
4. Select pickets to highlight with roofs. Cut wood for roofs and attach.
5. Use hole saw in posts to create "entrance holes" on some posts.
6. Drill holes for dowel perches. Cut dowels. Coat one end with glue and insert dowels in holes. Let dry.
7. Paint "roofs" and "birdhouses" with the colors of your choice. Let dry. ❏

Rose Watering Can

By Holly Buttimer

SUPPLIES

Project Surface:

Galvanized metal watering can

Paints & Finishes:

Acrylic craft paint

Black	Burgundy
Fresh Foliage	Light Blue
Lime	Magenta
Olive	Orange
Pink	Tangerine
White	Yellow

Indoor/outdoor gloss acrylic enamel paint

Damask Blue

Acrylic sealer

Tools & Other Supplies:

Artist paint brushes

Rubbing alcohol

Sea sponge

INSTRUCTIONS

Prepare & Base Paint:

1. Wipe can with rubbing alcohol.
2. Paint can with Damask Blue. Let dry.
3. Dampen sponge and pounce in Light Blue. Sponge the can randomly. Let dry.
4. Transfer the pattern.

Paint the Design:

Roses

1. Paint with Pink.
2. Shade with Magenta and highlight with White, making circular strokes to give the look of petals.

Leaves

1. Paint with Fresh Foliage.

Patterns

Enlarge patterns @ 145% for actual size.

2. Highlight with Lime. Shade with Olive.
3. Add strokes of Magenta here and there.

Butterfly

1. Paint with Orange.
2. Highlight with Yellow and Tangerine.

3. Shade with Burgundy.
4. Outline and detail wings with Black. Add White dots.
5. Paint body with Black. Highlight with White.

Finish:

Seal with acrylic sealer. Let dry. ❏

Garden Elf Slate

By Holly Buttimer

SUPPLIES

Project Surface:

Slate, size 14" x 16" or size to fit your pattern

Paints & Finishes:

Acrylic craft paints

Black

Buckskin

Burgundy

Burnt Sienna

Fresh Foliage

Gold (metallic)

Light Blue

Lime

Olive

Orange

Peridot (metallic)

Pink

Poppy Red

Red

Rose Beige

Tangerine

White

Yellow

Acrylic sealer

Tools & Other Supplies:

Artist paint brushes

INSTRUCTIONS

Prepare:

1. Paint slate with Light Blue. Let dry.
2. Transfer pattern.

Paint the Design:

Face, Ears & Hair

1. Paint with Rose Beige.
2. Paint cheeks with Pink.
3. Shade face and ears with Burgundy and Buckskin. Highlight with White.
4. Paint lips with Red and Burgundy.
5. Paint hair with Buckskin. Shade with Burnt Sienna and Gold. Highlight with White.

Hat & Mushroom Stool

1. Paint hat and mushroom cap with Red. Shade with Burgundy. Highlight with Poppy Red.
2. Add White dots to hat and mushroom cap.
3. Paint mushroom stem with White. Shade with Light Blue, gray (a mix of Black and White), and Gold.
4. Shade along bottom of mushroom with Gold.
5. Outline mushroom and hat with Black.

Shirt, Pants & Shoes

1. Paint shirt with Fresh Foliage. Highlight with Lime. Shade with a mix of Lime and Peridot.
2. Paint pants and shoes with Buckskin. Shade with Burnt Sienna. Highlight with strokes of Gold and White.

Butterfly

1. Paint wings with Orange. Highlight with Tangerine and Yellow. Shade with Gold.
2. Add details to wings with Black and White.
3. Paint body and antennae with Black. Highlight with White.

Flowers & Foliage

1. Paint grass blades with all the shades of green – Fresh Foliage, Olive, Peridot, and Lime.
2. Paint daisy petals with White.
3. Paint daisy centers with Yellow, Tangerine, and Orange.

Bee

1. Paint body with Black and Yellow stripes.
2. Highlight with White and Gold.
3. Paint wings with White. Shade with Light Blue.
4. Outline and add antennae with Black. Let dry.

Finish:

Seal with acrylic sealer. Let dry. ❑

Pattern for
Garden Elf Slate

Enlarge pattern @165%
for actual size.

Instructions appear
on page 72.

Pattern for Rose-Covered Birdhouse

(actual size)

Instructions appear on page 76.

Rose-Covered Birdhouse

By Holly Buttimer

SUPPLIES

Project Surface:

Wooden birdhouse

Paints & Finishes:

Acrylic craft paints
(see color chart for list of colors)
Clear acrylic sealer

Tools & Other Supplies:

Artist paint brushes

INSTRUCTIONS

Base Paint:

1. Base paint with Lemonade.
2. Add Burgundy stripes to sides. Highlight stripes with Pink.
3. Add stripes of Buttercup along each Burgundy stripe.
4. Transfer pattern.

Paint the Design:

Flowers & Leaves

1. Paint roses with strokes of Burgundy, Alizarin Crimson, Magenta, and Pink.
2. Paint leaves with shades of green – Fresh Foliage, Olive, and Lime.
3. Paint aster petals with Periwinkle. Shade with Dark Purple. Highlight with White.
4. Paint aster centers with Orange.
5. Add strokes of Periwinkle to leaves here and there.

Butterfly

1. Paint butterfly wings with White.

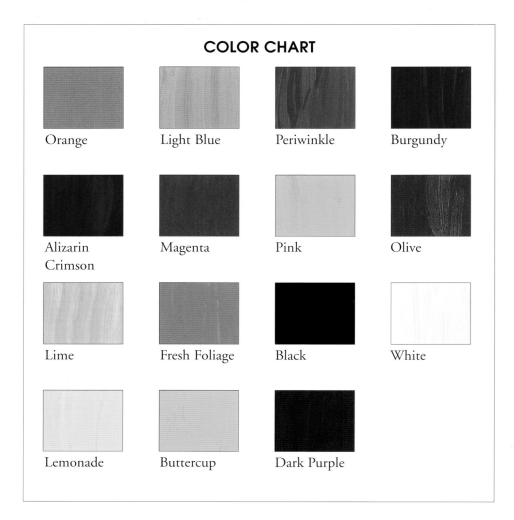

COLOR CHART

Orange	Light Blue	Periwinkle	Burgundy
Alizarin Crimson	Magenta	Pink	Olive
Lime	Fresh Foliage	Black	White
Lemonade	Buttercup	Dark Purple	

Add Orange dots. Shade with Gold.

2. Paint body, outlines, and antennae with Black.

Bee

1. Paint bee's body with Black.
2. Add Yellow stripes. Highlight with White.
3. Paint wings with White.
4. Outline with Black.

Finish:

Seal with acrylic sealer.

Wild Roosters Bench

By Holly Buttimer

SUPPLIES

Project Surface:

Wooden bench

Paints & Finishes:

Acrylic craft paint

  Black

  Buckskin

  Burgundy

  Fresh Foliage

  Gold (metallic)

  Golden Yellow

  Light Blue

  Lime

  Magenta

  Olive

  Orange

  Periwinkle

  Poppy Red

  Red

  Sea Green

  Tangerine

  True Blue

  White

  Yellow

Clear acrylic sealer

Tools & Other Supplies:

Sandpaper

Artist paint brushes

Combing tool

INSTRUCTIONS

Prepare & Base Paint:

1. Sand bench smooth with sandpaper. Wipe away dust.
2. Base edges of legs and top with Lime.
3. Transfer shape of inset to top.
4. Paint inside inset with Black.
5. Paint sides of legs and area on top outside of inset with Lemonade.
6. Paint leg braces with Light Blue. Let dry.
7. Brush Olive paint on edges of legs and top. Comb with the combing tool to create stripes.
8. Paint area outside of inset with Sea Green. Comb with the combing tool to create stripes. On outsides of legs, randomly brush Buckskin. Let dry.
9. Transfer the design.

Paint the Design:

Leopard Spots

1. Paint spots with Buckskin and brown (a mix of Buckskin and Burgundy).
2. Outline with Black.
3. Highlight with Gold.

Roosters

1. Paint rooster feathers with Golden Yellow.
2. Shade with Buckskin and Burgundy, using more of these colors to create the feathers of the rooster on the left.
3. Highlight feathers with Gold, White, and Yellow.
4. Paint beaks with Yellow. Highlight with White. Shade with Gold.
5. Paint combs, wattles, and area around eyes with Red. Shade with Burgundy. Highlight with White and Poppy Red.

Continued on page 80

continued from page 78

6. Paint eyes with Yellow with Black pupils and White highlights.

Daisies
1. Paint petals with White.
2. Paint centers with Yellow and Orange.
3. Paint leaves with Fresh Foliage. Highlight with Lime. Shade with Olive.

Blue Butterfly
1. Paint wings of one butterfly with Light Blue. Shade and add details with Periwinkle and True Blue.
2. Paint body with Black. Highlight with White.

Orange Butterflies
1. Paint other butterflies' wings with Orange and Tangerine.
2. Shade with Poppy Red. Highlight with Yellow and edge with White. Trim with Black.
3. Paint body with Black. Highlight with White.

Yellow Butterfly
1. Paint wings with Yellow.
2. Shade with Buckskin.
3. Accent with Black.
4. Edge wings with White and paint body and antennae with White.

Strawberry
1. Paint with Red.
2. Highlight with Poppy Red, Magenta, and White. Shade with Burgundy.
3. Paint bracts with Fresh Foliage. Highlight with Lime. Shade with Olive.
4. Dot seeds with Black.

Ladybug
1. Paint with Red and Black.
2. Shade with Burgundy. Highlight with White.
3. Paint legs, outlines, and antennae with White. Let dry.

Finish:
1. Outline inset with Golden Yellow. Shade with Buckskin. Let dry.
2. Seal with acrylic sealer. Let dry. ❑

Pattern for Leopard Spots
on bench sides
(actual size)

Pattern for Rooster Bench Top

Enlarge patterns @ 125% for actual size.

Butterfly Door Mat

What a beautiful floorcloth to place on porch or front door entrance. You can use it outdoors if it is well coated with outdoor sealer. To keep it looking good, it is best to keep it in a protected area like a covered porch to protect it from weather.

By Holly Buttimer

SUPPLIES

Project Surface:
Primed canvas floorcloth

Paints & Finishes:
Acrylic craft paints
  Alizarin Crimson
  Black
  Buckskin
  Fresh Foliage
  Gold (metallic)
  Lemonade
  Light Blue
  Lime
  Olive
  Periwinkle
  Pink
  Red
  True Blue
  Turquoise
  White
  Yellow
Clear acrylic sealer

Tools & Other Supplies:
Artist paint brushes
Painter's masking tape
Sea sponge

INSTRUCTIONS

Paint Background:
1. Mask off inside area of canvas. Paint with periwinkle. Let dry.
2. Sponge with Light Blue, then True Blue to create a mottled, textured look. Remove tape. Let dry completely.
3. Mask off the border. See Fig. 1 for measurements. Paint the long sides with Pink. Paint the short sides with Fresh Foliage. Paint the corners with Black. Remove tape. Let dry.
4. Lightly sponge green borders with Olive, then White. Let dry.
5. Paint area outside borders with peach (Red + Lemonade).
6. Transfer patterns.

Paint the Designs:
Sunflowers
1. Paint petals with Yellow. Highlight with Buckskin.
2. Paint centers with Gold. Add dots with Buckskin and White.
3. Add detailing with Black.

Border with Vines
1. Paint the leafy vines on the green border areas with Olive. Let dry.
2. Sponge a little peach (a mix of Red and Lemonade) here and there.

Continued on page 84

continued from page 82

Border with Plaid

Paint a plaid on the pink border areas, making vertical wide brush strokes with Turquoise, narrow vertical brush strokes with White, and narrow horizontal strokes with True Blue and Yellow.

Butterfly

1. Paint wings with Yellow and Black.
2. Highlight with Lemonade and White. Shade with Gold.
3. Add Periwinkle and Light Blue spots and Red spots at the bottom.
4. Paint the body with Black. Highlight with White and Gold.
5. Add details with Gold. Let dry.

Finish:

Seal with two or three coats of acrylic sealer. Let dry. ❑

Fig. 1 - Measurements for Border

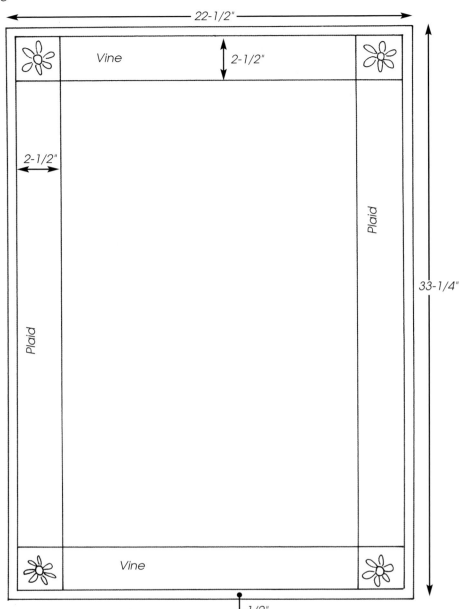

Patterns for Borders, Corner Motifs
(actual size)

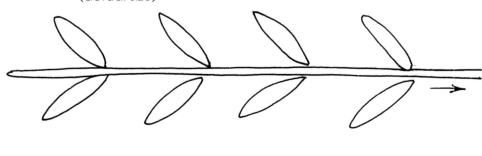

Pattern for Butterfly

Enlarge pattern @ 175% for actual size.

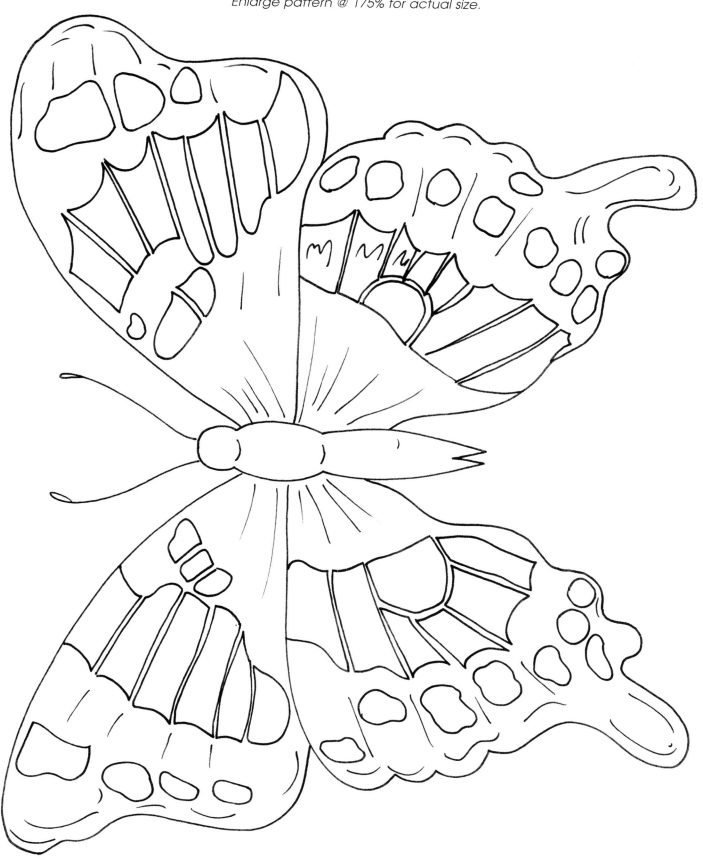

Painted Cottage Rocks

These painted rocks, painted to look like cottages for garden
fairies, add a whimsical touch to the border of garden beds
or paths. Look for rocks with smooth surfaces at garden
centers and hardware stores that sell landscaping supplies.

By Holly Buttimer

SUPPLIES

Project Surface:

Rocks

Paints & Finishes:

Acrylic craft paints
  (see color chart for list of colors)
Clear acrylic sealer

Tools & Other Supplies:

Artist paint brushes

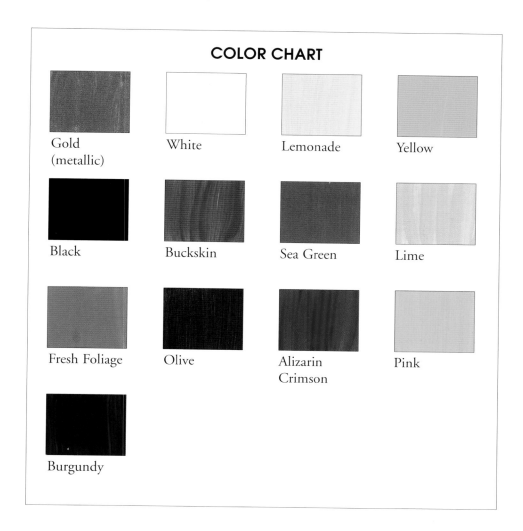

COLOR CHART

Gold (metallic)	White	Lemonade	Yellow
Black	Buckskin	Sea Green	Lime
Fresh Foliage	Olive	Alizarin Crimson	Pink
Burgundy			

INSTRUCTIONS

Prepare:
Transfer the door and window shapes to your rock.

Paint the Design:
1. Choose a color for the "walls" of your cottage – the larger rock here has Sea Green walls, the smaller one has walls of Pink shaded with Burgundy.
2. Paint thatched roof with Yellow. Highlight with Lemonade and White. Shade with Buckskin, Burgundy, and Gold.
3. Paint door and windows with White. Paint window panes with Yellow or yellow gold (a mix of Yellow and Alizarin Crimson). Outline and add details with Black.
4. Paint greenery around the bottom edge with Fresh Foliage. Highlight with Lime and shade with Olive.
5. Add flowers of various colors – Pink, Alizarin Crimson, Yellow, orange (a mix of Lemonade and Alizarin Crimson). Let dry.

Finish:
Seal with acrylic sealer. Let dry. ❑

Patterns for Painted Cottage Rocks

Instructions appear on page 87.

(actual size)

Pattern for Rabbit Pillow

Instructions appear on page 90.

Enlarge pattern @165% for actual size.

Rabbit Pillow

By Holly Buttimer

SUPPLIES

Project Surface:

Pillow cover   Pillow form

Paints & Mediums:

Acrylic craft paints

(see color chart for list of colors)

Textile Medium

Tools & Other Supplies:

Artist paint brushes

Iron

Clothes dryer

Cardboard

Plastic wrap

Masking tape

INSTRUCTIONS

Prepare:

1. Wash and dry pillow cover according to manufacturer's instructions. Press smooth.
2. Cut a piece of cardboard to fit inside pillow cover. Cover cardboard with plastic wrap and tape to secure. Place plastic-covered cardboard inside pillow.
3. Transfer pattern (page 89).
4. Mix paints and textile medium according to textile medium manufacturer's instructions.

Paint the Design:

1. Paint background with Light Blue.

Continued on page 92

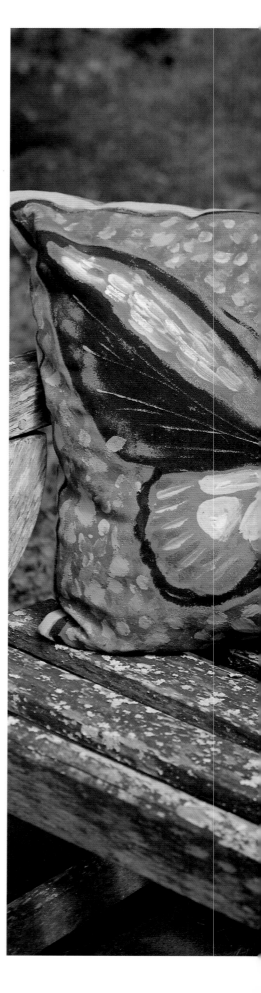

COLOR CHART

Light Blue	Black	Pink	Burgundy
Yellow	Buckskin	Orange	Tangerine
Fresh Foliage	Gold (metallic)	Peridot (metallic)	Lime
Sea Green	Olive	White	Gray

continued from page 90

2. Paint rabbit shape with White and Black. Shade with Gray.

3. Paint inside ears with Pink. Shade with Burgundy.

4. Paint eyes with Buckskin. Paint pupils with Black. Highlight with White.

5. Paint flower pot with Orange. Shade with Buckskin and Burgundy. Highlight with Tangerine, Gold, and White.

6. Paint grass in shades of green – Fresh Foliage, Lime, Olive, and Peridot.

7. Paint soil in pot with Black. Highlight with Olive and Lime.

8. Paint daisy petals with White. Paint daisy centers with Yellow and Orange.

9. Paint butterfly's wings with Orange. Shade with Burgundy. Highlight with Yellow and Tangerine. Add details with Black and White dots.

10. Paint bee's body with Black and Yellow. Shade with Gold. Highlight with White.

11. Paint bee's wings with White. Shade with Light Blue.

12. Outline rabbit's whiskers and add details with Black and White.

13. Paint the edge of the pillow with Lime. Let dry completely.

Finish:

Remove plastic-covered cardboard from pillow. Turn pillow inside out. Heat set by tumbling in dryer. Let cool. Place form inside pillow. ❑

Butterfly Pillow

Pictured on page 91

By Holly Buttimer

SUPPLIES

Project Surface:

Pillow cover

Pillow form

Paints & Mediums:

Acrylic craft paints

Black

Buckskin

Gold (metallic)

Lemonade

Orange

Pale Peach

Periwinkle

Sea Green

Turquoise

White

Textile Medium

Tools & Other Supplies:

Artist paint brushes

Iron

Clothes dryer

Cardboard

Plastic wrap

Masking tape

INSTRUCTIONS

Prepare:

1. Wash and dry pillow cover according to manufacturer's instructions. Press smooth.

2. Cut a piece of cardboard to fit inside pillow cover. Cover cardboard with plastic wrap and tape to secure. Place plastic-covered cardboard inside pillow.

3. Transfer pattern.

4. Mix paints and textile medium according to textile medium manufacturer's instructions.

Paint the Design:

1. Paint the background with Periwinkle.

2. Paint butterfly's wings and body with Buckskin and Black, using the photo as a guide for placement. Let dry.

3. Paint the outer edge of the pillow with Pale Peach.

4. Add dabs on the background with Sea Green, Turquoise, and Pale Peach.

5. Add highlights and details on the wings and body with Pale Peach, Gold, Lemonade, Black, Periwinkle, and White. Let dry completely.

Finish:

Remove plastic-covered cardboard from pillow. Turn pillow inside out. Heat set by tumbling in dryer. Let cool. Place form inside pillow. ❑

Pattern for Butterfly Pillow

Enlarge pattern @ 170% for actual size.

Concrete Stepping Stones

Painted stepping stones can enliven garden beds and add
whimsy and color (as well as providing a place to step). Use one
alone as a focal point, place them in pairs or trios, or group them
to create a path, depending on your space. Selecting a single
background color (like the light blue here) on all the stones in
a group will create a unified look.
Concrete stepping stones are widely available in a variety of sizes and
shapes (typically round, square, or octagonal) at garden centers and
hardware stores.

By Holly Buttimer

SUPPLIES

Project Surface:
Concrete stepping stone(s)

Paints & Finishes:
Acrylic craft paints
See the patterns for the colors used.
Outdoor sealer

Tools & Other Supplies:
Artist paint brushes

BASIC INSTRUCTIONS

1. Be sure the stone is clean and dry.
   Base paint with your chosen color
   (here, Light Blue). Let dry.
2. Transfer the design.
3. Paint the design, using the colors
   noted and the photos as guides. Let
   dry.
4. Seal with several coats of outdoor
   sealer. ❏

Pictured above: Bunny Stepping Stone.

Pictured at right top to bottom: Bumblebee Stepping Stone, Frog Stepping Stone,
Bird's Nest Stepping Stone, Ladybug Stepping Stone, Bunny Stepping Stone.

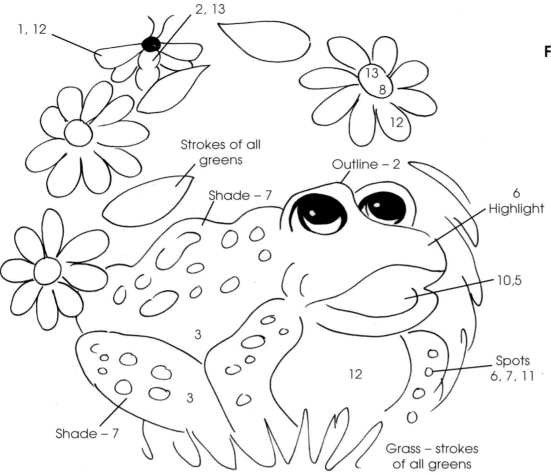

2, 13

1, 12

Frog Stepping Stone

1. Buckskin
2. Black
3. Fresh Foliage
4. Light Blue
5. Light Pink
6. Lime
7. Olive
8. Orange
9. Peridot (metallic)
10. Red
11. Sea Green
12. White
13. Yellow

Background = 4

Strokes of all greens

Shade – 7

Outline – 2

6 Highlight

13
8

12

10,5

3

12

Spots 6, 7, 11

3

Shade – 7

Grass – strokes of all greens

Enlarge patterns to fit the size of your stone.

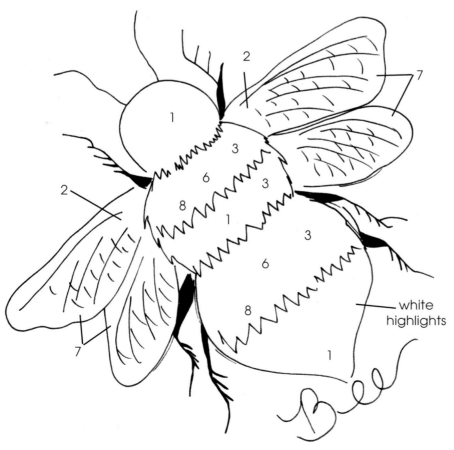

1

2

3

6

3

8

1

3

6

8

1

2

7

7

7

white highlights

1

Bee

Bumblebee Stepping Stone

1. Black
2. Lavender
3. Lemonade
4. Light Blue
5. Lime
6. Tangerine
7. White
8. Yellow

Background = 4

Border = 5, 2 lavender

Details = 1

Background = 6

Shade –
3

5, 3

5

2

Shade – 6

12

Strokes
of 13, 9,
11, 2

black

11, 13

12

Grass = strokes
of all greens

Enlarge patterns to fit the size of your stone.

Bunny Stepping Stone

1. Black
2. Buckskin
3. Burgundy
4. Fresh Foliage
5. Light Pink
6. Light Blue
7. Lime
8. Olive
9. Orange
10. Peridot (metallic)
11. Tangerine
12. White
13. Yellow

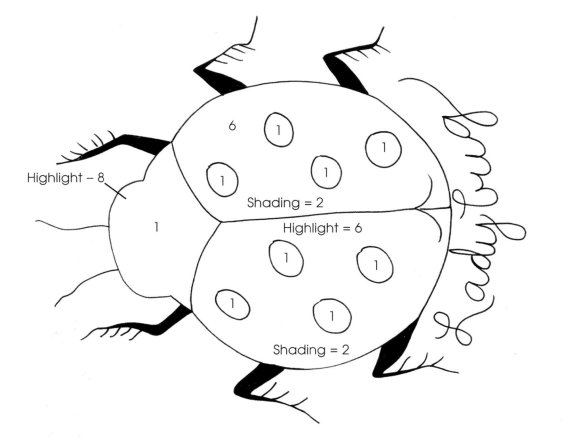

6

1

1

1

1

Highlight – 8

1

Shading = 2

Highlight = 6

1

1

1

1

Shading = 2

Ladybug
Stepping Stone

1. Black
2. Burgundy
3. Lavender
4. Light Blue
5. Lime
6. Poppy Red
7. Red
8. White

Background = 4

Border = 5, 3

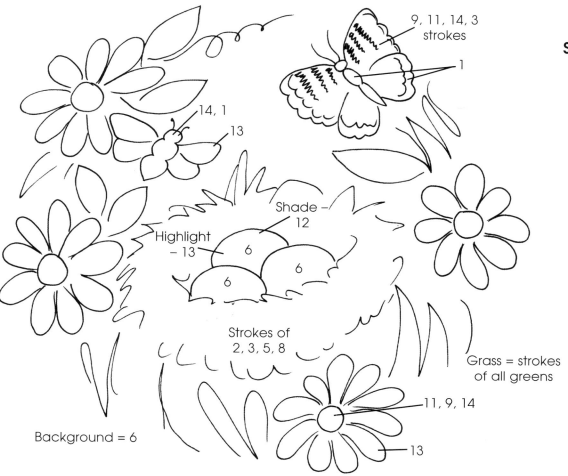

9, 11, 14, 3
strokes

1

14, 1

13

Shade –
12

Highlight
– 13

6

6

6

Strokes of
2, 3, 5, 8

Grass = strokes
of all greens

11, 9, 14

13

Background = 6

Bird's Nest Stepping Stone

1. Black
2. Buckskin
3. Burnt Sienna
4. Fresh Foliage
5. Gold (metallic)
6. Light Blue
7. Lime
8. Mushroom
9. Orange
10. Peridot (metallic)
11. Tangerine
12. True Blue
13. White
14. Yellow

MOSAICS
FOR
YOUR GARDEN

Because mosaic pieces usually use tile, these pieces
are very durable in the garden. Mosaics can
be a bright and creative addition to your garden.
And the best part is, mosaics are easy to
make – most projects can be completed in an
afternoon. The mosaic technique requires
very few materials – a quick visit to your hardware
store will reap all the supplies you need.

Pictured at right: Fish Mosaic Table Top. See page 104 for instructions.

Mosaic Supplies

Project Surface

You can create mosaics using almost any smooth and stable surface as a base. Mosaics look great added to concrete pieces such as stepping stones; to wood surfaces such as table tops or plaques; to terra cotta flower pots; or even to metal objects like mailboxes.

Tile Pieces or Tesserae

You can use pieces of tile – broken or whole. You can also use broken pieces of glass, china, pottery; or even found objects like shells, stones, metal objects. These pieces are glued onto a surface to create a design.

Tools

You will need a **rubber mallet or hammer, newspapers, and safety glasses** when breaking the tile pieces. After you break the pieces, you can use **tile nippers** to cut the pieces smaller or trim them to fit. A **rubber spatula, small nylon trowel, or putty knife** is needed for spreading the grout onto the surface. A **sponge** is needed for grout cleanup.

Glue

To assemble your mosaics you will need an all-purpose, heavy duty glue to attach the mosaic pieces to the project surface.

Grout

After all the pieces are glued into place, you will fill in the spaces between the pieces with tile grout. You can use pre-mixed grout or a dry grout, mixing it with water until it is an icing consistency. Grout can be tinted with special grout colorings or with acrylic paint.

Finish

After the grout has dried, you can seal your project for outdoor use with an outdoor sealer.

Mosaic Technique

The technique for creative mosaic projects is very easy:

1. Plan your design and pencil the design onto your surface.
2. Prepare your surface. Make sure it is clean, dry, and smooth. If you are using a wood surface, be sure to seal it with an outdoor sealer.
3. Prepare the mosaic pieces. Purchase enough square inches of tile to create your design. If you desire, you can break larger tile squares into smaller pieces by placing them between layers of newspaper and hitting with a mallet or hammer.
4. Glue the tile pieces to your surface using heavy duty glue. Allow to dry.
5. Spread grout over the surface, pushing it into the spaces between the mosaic pieces.
6. Wipe off excess grout with a damp sponge. Keep wiping until all the white residue is gone. Wait 10 minutes. If you see white residue then wipe away with damp sponge or cloth. Buff with a dry, soft cloth. ❑

Pattern for Fish Mosaic Table Top

(actual size)

Instructions appear on page 104.

Fish Mosaic Table Top

This table top was so much fun and easy to make. It was constructed
on a piece of plywood then place atop an existing wrought
iron base that was rescued from the basement. For this design, choose
a tinted grout to match the grout of the purchased mosaic or add
acrylic paint in coordinating color to white grout.

By Kathi Malarchuk Bailey

SUPPLIES

Project Surface:

Plywood or 1/4" hardboard, 18" square

Sea shells and small stones

12 dark blue glazed tiles, 5" square

Orange glazed tile, 6" square

Colbalt blue glazed tile with yellow trim, 6" square

Scrap pieces of turquoise tile

Tools & Other Supplies:

Waterproof glue

Grout, *ours was tinted with black paint*

Tile nippers

Hammer or mallet

Newspapers

Safety glasses

Cellulose sponge

Small trowel or putty knife

Plastic scraper

Sandpaper

Grout sealer

Optional: Clear sealer (if using plywood); Black acrylic paint (for tinting grout)

INSTRUCTIONS

Prepare:

1. Sand edges of plywood or hardboard to smooth. Seal plywood with clear sealer to prevent warping.
2. To break tiles, place three or four tiles on newspapers on a hard surface. Cover with additional newspapers. Wearing safety glasses, use a hammer to break the tiles into smaller pieces. Continue until all tiles are broken into smaller pieces.

Note: We found a cobalt blue tile with yellow trim. When it was broken, we tried to keep the pieces in place so they could be used to create the outside edge of the fish centerpiece square.

Glue:

1. Mark off a 6" square in the center of the plywood board. Also draw or transfer the fish pattern in the center of this square.
2. Glue down the cobalt and yellow edge pieces all around the marked line.
3. Glue the orange tile pieces in place to create the fish shape. Add a piece of cobalt and the scrap of turquoise for the eye.
4. Fill in around the fish with more cobalt blue pieces.
5. Position and adhere shells and stones to create a border for the centerpiece. Glue a shell at each outer corner.
6. Use broken dark blue tile pieces to fill in the remaining background areas.
7. Allow to dry overnight.

Note: Break tiles with a tile nipper to fit them into the design.

Grout:

1. Prepare grout in disposable container according to manufacturer's instructions. *If a tinted grout is desired,* add enough coordinating acrylic paint (in this case, Black) to achieve a shade two times darker than the desired shade. (The grout color will lighten as it dries.)
2. Place mosaic panel on newspaper and/or plastic sheet. Apply grout with a trowel, ensuring that the entire top area and sides are covered. Use a plastic scraper to push grout around and down into the spaces between the tiles, shells, and stones. Scrape diagonally across the entire surface to fill spaces. Allow to set up for approximately 15 minutes.

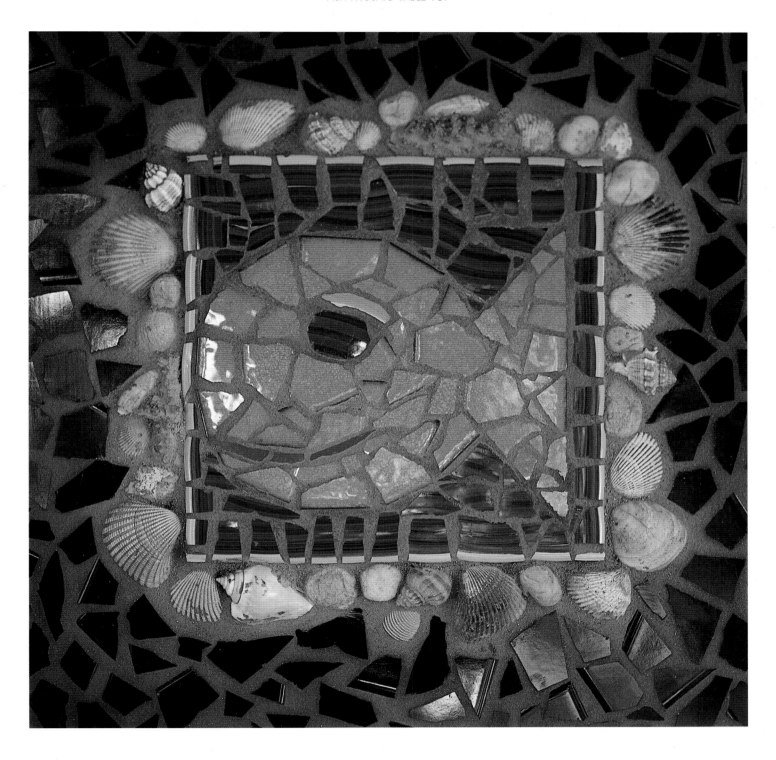

3. Fill bucket with clean water. Wearing rubber gloves, dampen sponge and start wiping off grout. Rinse the sponge in the bucket and replace the water regularly. Continue until all of grout is removed from top of tiles. Let dry. (A haze will appear on the tile as it dries.)

4. Wipe off the haze with clean, damp sponge until tile is clear. Allow to dry thoroughly to cure.

5. Seal grout to prevent water damage. ❏

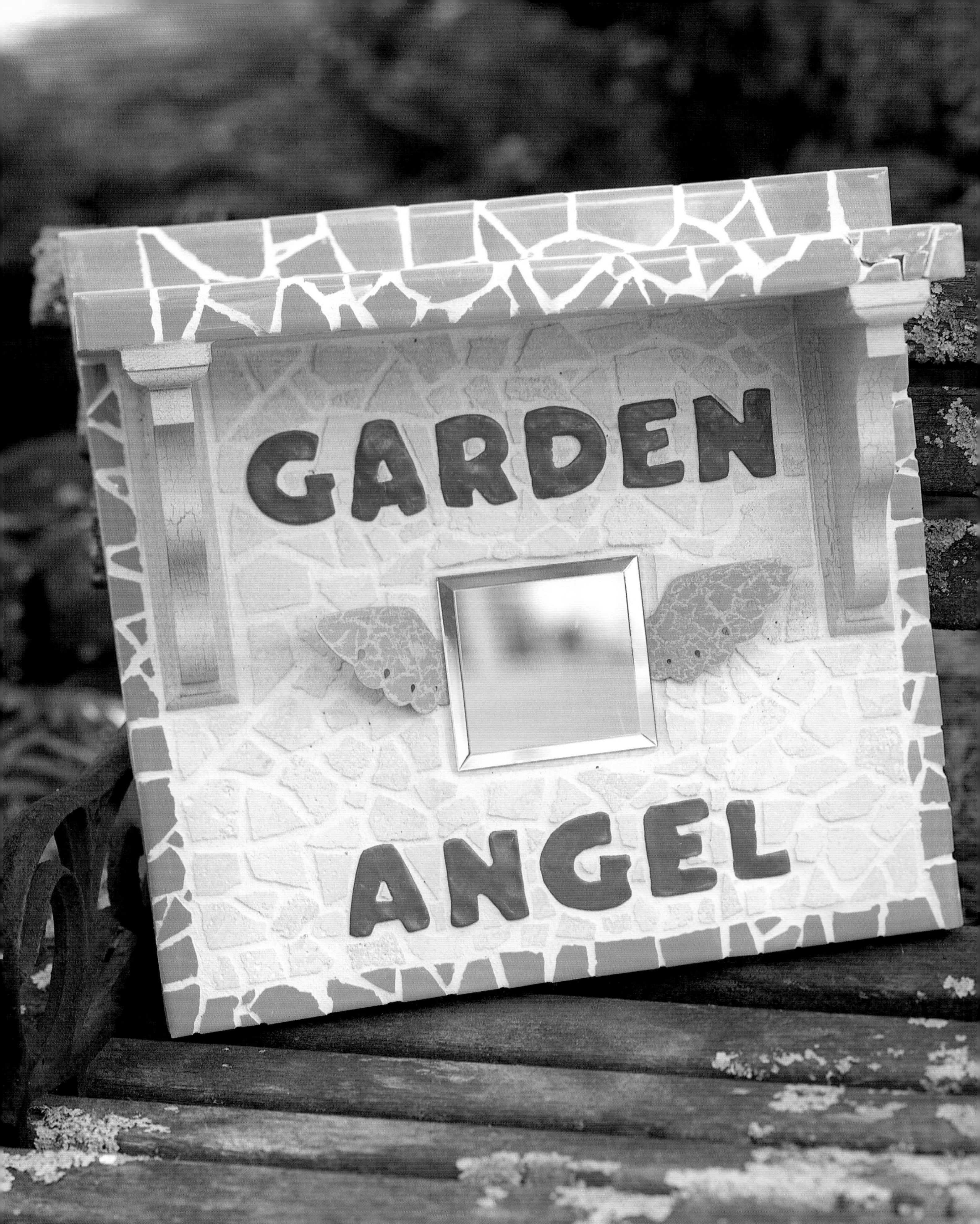
GARDEN
ANGEL

Garden Shelf & Mirror

By Patty Cox

SUPPLIES

Project Surface:

Plywood, 3/4" thick - 16" x 16" (for back), 16" x 5" (for shelf)

2 wooden corner brackets, 5" x 7"

Blue-green tiles

Off white marble tiles

Polymer clay - terra cotta color

Paints, Mediums & Finishes:

Acrylic craft paints

    Off White

    Mint Green

Crackle medium

Clear polyurethane spray finish

Tools & Other Supplies:

4" square beveled mirror

1 pair metal wings

Sandpaper

Alphabet cookie cutters *or* pattern for letters (provided)

Hammer or mallet

Tile nippers

Safety glasses

Small trowel or putty knife

Saw

Grout, white

Sponge

Clear-drying multi-purpose, industrial strength glue

Paint brush

Heavy duty hanging bracket

Wax paper

Rolling pin

Newspaper

Large craft stick *or* plastic putty knife

Making terra cotta letters from polymer clay.

INSTRUCTIONS

Make the Shelf:

1. Sand wood pieces.
2. Assemble shelf on plywood backing with corner brackets, positioning shelf 2-1/2" below top edge and brackets 3/4" from each side.
3. Attach hanging bracket to shelf back.

Make Terra Cotta Letters:

1. Place clay on wax paper.
2. Lay two tiles to the right and left side of clay to act as a thickness guide. Place another sheet of wax paper over clay. Use rolling pin to roll over clay, resting the edges of the rolling pin on the tiles so the clay will be the same thickness as the tile.
3. Use cookie cutters to cut letters from clay *or* use patterns provided to cut letters.
4. Bake letters in oven 15 minutes. Let cool.
5. Spray tops of letters with clear polyurethane finish.

Paint & Crackle Shelf:

1. Paint the underside of the shelf and the brackets with Mint Green. Let dry.
2. Paint side edges of the shelf, the backing board edges, and the metal wings with Off White. Let dry.
3. Brush crackle medium on painted areas. Let dry according to manufacturer's instructions.
4. Brush over green-painted areas with Off White paint. Brush off-white areas with Mint Green. Cracks will form. Let dry.
5. Spray painted surfaces with clear polyurethane finish.

Continued on page 108

continued form page 107

Create the Mosaic:

1. Pencil a 3/4" border around the sides of the backing board. Mark placement lines for the letters and mirror.
2. Glue letters in place with adhesive. Glue a whole 4" tile where you will be placing the mirror.
3. Place tiles between several layers of newspaper on a concrete surface. Break tiles with hammer.
4. Glue pieces of blue-green tiles on shelf top and outer edge, on backing board above shelf, and along 3/4" border. Use tile nippers as needed to shape tiles.
5. Glue off white tiles around lettering and inside the blue-green border. Allow glue to dry.
6. Using a small trowel or putty knife, apply white grout over mosaic design, pressing the grout between the tile pieces.
7. Wipe mosaic design with a damp sponge. Wipe grout away from center 4" tile. Allow grout to dry.

Add Wings & Mirror:
Glue wings and beveled mirror in position on center 4" tile.
❏

Pattern for Wings
(actual size)

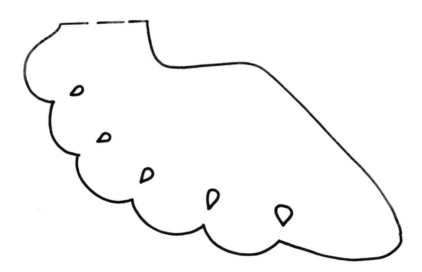

Note: If you can't find pre-cut metal wings, use this
pattern to cut your own from thin copper or tin sheeting.
Tin and copper sheeting that can be cut with scissors or
a craft knife is available at many craft shops.

Pattern for Alphabet

Enlarge to size needed.

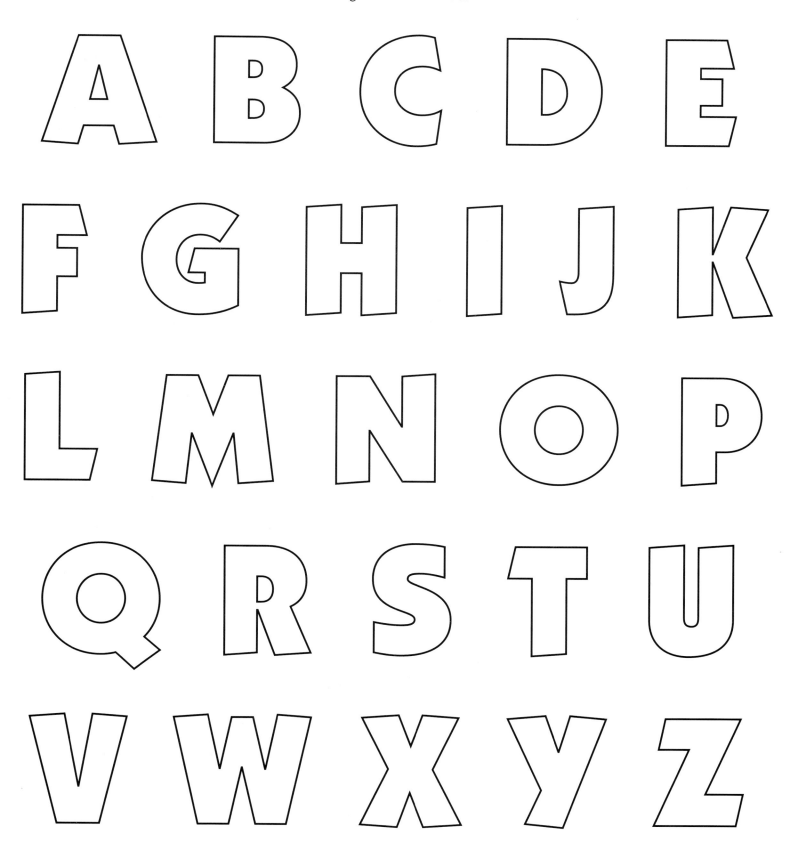

Mosaic Turtle

This sand-cast cement turtle shape is easy to make. Pebbles and gravel are pressed into premixed tile adhesive and grout to form the mosaic design.

By Patty Cox

SUPPLIES

Project Surface:

Portland cement

Black pebbles

Pea gravel, red-brown, white, and gray

Tools & Other Supplies:

Pre-mixed tile adhesive and sanded grout combination, antique white

Large oval aluminum roasting pan

Sand

Oval bowl

Round soup ladle

Craft sticks

Dust mask

Instructions follow on page 112.

continued from page 110

INSTRUCTIONS

Make the Cement Base:

1. Fill roasting pan about three-quarters full of sand.
2. Press an oval bowl impression in center of sand.
3. Using a ladle, scoop out sand from head, feet, and tail areas to make a turtle shape.
4. Remove bowl. Using your finger, smooth flat or irregular areas of sand.
5. Wearing a dust mask, mix cement according to package instructions. Pour into turtle impression in sand. (**Photo 1**) Let dry completely.
6. Remove turtle shape. Scrub off excess sand. (**Photo 2**)

Create the Mosaic:

Work one area at a time as you create the mosaic design.

1. Apply tile adhesive and grout mixture to turtle's back, using a craft stick.
2. Using the photos as guides for placement, press black pebbles in adhesive grout. (**Photo 3**)
3. Press gray pea gravel in grout between black pebbles.
4. Press an oval row of red-brown pea gravel around the black pebble design.
5. Apply adhesive grout to an area about 3" wide on the side of the turtle.
6. Press a row of white pea gravel in a row along the turtle's bottom edge.
7. Fill side area in with gray pea gravel.
8. Continue adding small areas of adhesive grout and gravel around the turtle's sides, head, and feet. Use pieces of red-brown gravel for the eyes. Let dry and cure. ❏

1. The turtle shape is pressed into the sand and cement is poured in.

2. When completely set up and dry, the turtle shape is removed from the sand.

3. One area at a time, the turtle shape is covered with premixed ceramic tile adhesive and grout. Pebbles and gravel are pressed into the wet adhesive/grout to create the mosaic design.

METAL ORNAMENTS

Metal is durable and weather-resistant, making it a perfect material for use outdoors. This section includes instructions for making sconces from sheet copper and aluminum windchimes.

Copper Sconces

By Patty Cox

SUPPLIES

Project Surface:

Copper metal sheeting

Tools & Other Supplies:

Tin snips or old scissors

Metal cement

Vise *or* a heavyweight straight edge

Rubber mallet

Nail or hole punch

Eyelets and punch

Pebbles (to use as weights)

Clothes pins

Optional (for patina finish):

Chlorine bleach

Vinegar

Disposable pan

Damp cloth (for wiping)

INSTRUCTIONS

Form the Sconce:

1. Cut sheet copper according to pattern.
2. Grip top edge of each piece in vise, 1/4" down. Bend copper edge. Remove from vise. Pound 1/4" folded lip flat with rubber mallet. Fold over each of the four top sections 1/4".
3. Grip sconce center front in vise grip. Bend copper. Grip each side and bend copper. See Photo 1.
4. Form triangle sconce, overlapping ends to form the back. See Photo 2.
5. Glue copper where the sections overlap. Secure top edge with clothespins.
6. Fill sconce with pebbles. Lay flat to hold overlap together while glue dries.

Add the Eyelet Hanger:

1. Punch a hole at center back in the overlapped copper, using a nail or a punch.
2. Set an eyelet in hole. See Photo 2.

Option: Patina Finish:

Left outdoors, the copper will – over time – develop a weathered patina.

Photo 1. Bending the copper in the vise.

Photo 2. Set an eyelet in the back section for hanging the sconce.

Pattern for Copper Sconces

Enlarge pattern @155% for actual size.

Instructions appear on page 115.

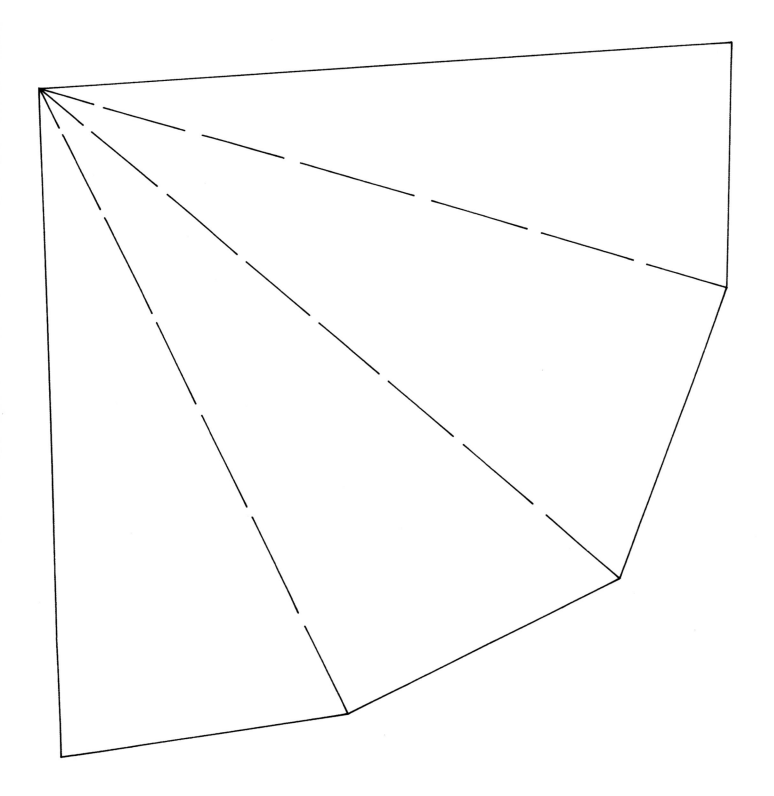

Bluebird Aluminum Wind Chimes
Construction Diagrams

Instructions appear on page 118.

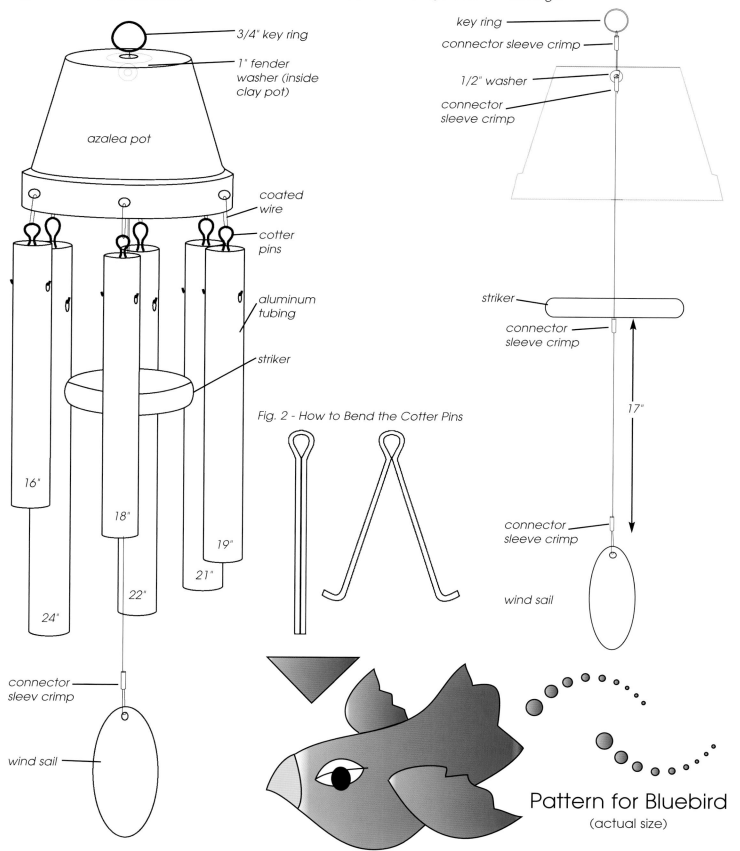

Fig. 1 - The Finished Windchime

3/4" key ring

1" fender washer (inside clay pot)

azalea pot

coated wire

cotter pins

aluminum tubing

striker

16"

18"

19"

21"

22"

24"

connector sleev crimp

wind sail

Fig. 2 - How to Bend the Cotter Pins

Fig. 3 - Attaching the Wind Sail, Striker & Hanger

key ring

connector sleeve crimp

1/2" washer

connector sleeve crimp

striker

connector sleeve crimp

17"

connector sleeve crimp

wind sail

Pattern for Bluebird
(actual size)

Bluebird Aluminum Wind Chimes

By Patty Cox

SUPPLIES

Project Surfaces:

Terra cotta azalea pot, 6-1/4"

10 ft. aluminum tubing, 1/2"

4" wooden disk (for striker)

3-1/2" wooden oval (for wind sail)

Paints & Finishes:

Indoor/outdoor gloss acrylic enamel paints

Black

Damask Blue

Green Mist

Light Blue

Mustard

White

Clear acrylic finish

Tools & Other Supplies:

Artist paint brushes

6 cotter pins, 2-1/2" (for tube hangers)

3/4" key ring (for top loop)

Drill and carbide bits

Pipe cutter

Hacksaw

Needlenose pliers

Nylon coated wire (30 lb. fishing line)

Connector sleeves (crimps for fishing line)

1" fender washer

1/2" washer

Pencil

Tape measure

Compressed sponge

Craft knife

INSTRUCTIONS

See the Construction Diagrams on page 117.

Drill Holes:

1. Measure rim of clay pot and divide into six equal parts. Pencil a dot on rim, 3/4" from lip edge. Mark six dots.
2. Using drill and 1/16" carbide bit, drill holes around rim at pencil dots. See Fig. 1.

Paint Clay Pot:

1. Base paint outside of pot and inner rim with White. Let dry.
2. Paint streaks of Light Blue, Damask Blue, and Green Mist around pot. Let dry.
3. Transfer three bluebird patterns around pot.
4. Paint birds with Light Blue.
5. Streak Green Mist on front of bird and wings. Streak Damask Blue on tail and backs of wings. Let dry.
6. Outline and paint bird details with Black, using a liner brush.
7. Using pattern provided, cut triangle from compressed sponge.
8. Dampen sponge. Sponge Damask Blue + Green Mist triangles around top edge of pot.
9. Using paint brush handle, dot curved flight lines between birds. Let dry.
10. Spray pot with clear finish. Let dry.

Add Chimes:

1. Using a pipe cutter, cut aluminum tubes into six lengths: 16", 18", 19", 21", 22", and 24".
2. Drill 3/16" holes through each pipe, 2" from one end.
3. Trim ends of cotter pins evenly with a hacksaw. Bend each end out at a 90 degree angle, using needlenose pliers. See Fig. 2.
4. Open cotter pin. Push inside end of aluminum tube where holes were drilled. (The bent ends of the cotter pins will snap into the holes in the tube.)
5. Attach one chime to each hole in clay pot with 6" coated wire. Crimp wire ends together inside pot. See Fig. 1.

Attach Wind Sail, Striker & Hanger:

See Fig. 3.

1. Glue a 1" fender washer inside clay pot, centering the washer over the drainage hole.
2. Drill a 1/16" hole in the center of the 4" wooden disk (the striker). Drill a 1/16" hole in one end of the 3-1/2" wooden oval (the wind sail).
3. Cut 36" of nylon coated wire. Thread a connector sleeve crimp on wire. Loop one end of wire through the hole in the wind sail. Slide crimp over wires. Secure crimp with pliers.
4. Thread another connector sleeve crimp on wire. Thread wooden disk (striker) on wire. Secure crimp (under disk) with pliers, about 17" above the wind sail.
5. Thread two connector sleeve crimps, a 1/2" metal washer, and the key ring on the end of the wire opposite the wind sail. Thread wire end through the drainage hole of the pot and the fender washer. Fold 4" of end wire over key ring. Crimp connector sleeve under key ring.
6. Thread 4" end wire back inside clay pot. Loop end wire through 1/2" washer. Crimp connector sleeve under loop. ❏

LANTERNS & LIGHTS

When darkness falls, the soft glow of lantern light and
candlelight can transform your garden into a magical place.
You can choose the objects and spaces you wish to illuminate,
letting others remain cloaked in darkness and mystery.
This section includes three projects that use recycled
materials – soft drink cans and wine bottles – and inexpensive
tea light candles to create lights that will lend glimmer and
glow to your garden in the dark and color and interest
in the daylight hours.

Can Lanterns

After cutting holes with a craft knife and scissors, aluminum soft drink cans from your recycle bin are painted with spray paint, then spattered with acrylic craft paints to make colorful garden lights.

By Patty Cox

SUPPLIES

Project Surface:

Aluminum soft drink cans

Paints:

Spray paints

    Boysenberry Pink   Lavender

    Lemon Yellow   Periwinkle

    Turquoise

Acrylic craft paint

    Boysenberry Pink   Lemon Yellow

    Periwinkle   Turquoise

Tools & Other Supplies:

Old toothbrush (for spattering)

Craft knife

Small scissors

Awl

Can opener

Fine tip permanent marker

17 gauge aluminum wire (for hangers – you need 18" for each can)

Tea light candles

Sand

12" piece of 1" diameter dowel

Round nose *or* needlenose pliers

Wire cutters

INSTRUCTIONS

Prepare:

1. Remove tops of cans using a can opener. Clean cans. Let dry.
2. Draw ovals around cans with a marker. Cut a pilot hole inside each oval, using a craft knife. Using scissors, cut out ovals.
3. Puncture two holes near the top of each can for the hanger wire.

Paint:

1. Spray paint outsides of cans with the colors listed. Let dry.

Tip: To prevent spray paint from getting on the insides of the cans, wrap a paper towel around a 1" dowel. Slide can over covered dowel, then spray.

2. Spatter cans with acrylic craft paints, using an old toothbrush. Here are the color combinations:

    Turquoise with Periwinkle spatters

    Periwinkle with Turquoise spatters

    Lavender with Turquoise spatters

    Lemon Yellow with Boysenberry Pink spatters

    Boysenberry Pink with Lemon Yellow spatters

Add Wire Hangers:

1. For each can, cut 18" of aluminum wire. Thread one end through one of the holes near the top of a can and form a coil 3" from the end, using round nose or needlenose pliers.
2. Wrap remaining wire around a pencil to make a coiled handle, leaving a 3" tail.
3. Thread tail through hole on opposite side of can. Coil end of wire around pliers.
4. Repeat for remaining cans.

Finish:

Pour about 1/4" of sand in the bottom of each can. Place one tea light candle in the sand in each can. ❏

Wine Bottle Lanterns

By Patty Cox

Beaded Wire Whisk Lantern

A wire whisk (this one cost less than a dollar at a discount store), decorated with beads, holds a tea light candle inside a cutoff wine bottle.

SUPPLIES

Wine bottle

Bottle cutter

Wire whisk

28 gauge wire

Assorted glass beads

Needlenose pliers

Tea light candle

Emery cloth

Plumber's putty

INSTRUCTIONS

Prepare:

1. Clean bottle, removing labels.
2. Using a bottle cutter, cut away lower 2" from bottom of bottle. Rub cut end with emery cloth to smooth.
3. Insert a tea light candle through wires of wire whisk.

Bead Whisk:

1. Cut a 2-yd. length of 28 gauge wire. Secure one end at whisk handle base. Thread glass beads on wire. Thread about a 3" length of beads on wire at a time. Spiral beaded wire around whisk. Wrap beaded wire around a whisk wire to secure. Continue

threading beads, spiral and securing beaded section around a whisk wire until all 2 yds. of wire have been beaded. Twist off the end of the wire. *Tip:* To thread beads on wire, pour glass beads in a shallow bowl. Holding wire about 2" from the end (as you would hold a needle), run wire end through the bowl of beads. Several beads will load each time the wire is swept through the beads.

2. Thread 24" of 28 gauge wire through wires on the balloon (bottom) part of the whisk. Pull ends evenly, then twist wires to secure. Thread beads on one 12" wire. Twist beads around one wire of whisk. Loop the end of the wire over a bead of the top wrapped section. Twist wire tail back around beaded wire returning to whisk bottom. Twist wire at whisk bottom center.
3. Repeat beaded twist on another whisk wire with the remaining 12" of 28 gauge wire. Wrap all 10 whisk wires. this way.
4. Hang a 4" strand of assorted glass beads from whisk bottom.

Assemble:

1. For added stability, press two or three straight pins through the wrapped wires into the sides of the tea light.
2. Press a small piece of plumber's putty into whisk handle top (this will keep moisture out).
3. Slide whisk handle through bottle top. ❏

Frosted Wine Bottle Lantern

Glass etching cream, available at hardware stores, makes a frosted pattern on a glass bottle. A tea light candle is suspended inside the bottle on coiled wire that was once an ordinary clothes hanger.

SUPPLIES

Wine bottle

Bottle cutter

Wire clothes hanger

1" wooden dowel

Pliers

Needlenose pliers

Self-adhesive paper

Glass etching cream

Old paintbrush

Tea light candle

Emery cloth

Craft knife

INSTRUCTIONS

Prepare:

1. Clean bottle, removing labels.
2. Using a bottle cutter, cut away lower 2" from bottom of bottle. Rub cut end with emery cloth to smooth.

Coil Wire:

See Fig. 1.

1. Cut top hook off hanger. Straighten remaining wire, using pliers. (Wire will be about 34" long.)

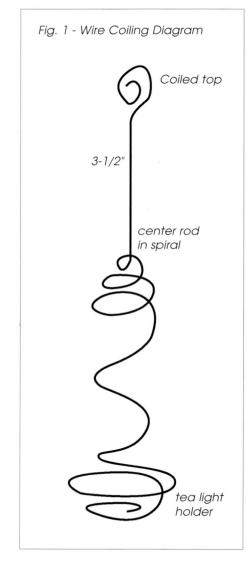

Fig. 1 - Wire Coiling Diagram

Coiled top

3-1/2"

center rod
in spiral

tea light
holder

2. Form a hanging loop in one end, using a needlenose pliers.
3. Measuring from the loop, leave 3-1/2" of wire straight, then wrap remaining wire around 1" dowel. Remove dowel.
4. Tighten the spiral top, centering the hanging loop.
5. Tighten spiral bottom just enough to hold a tea light candle. Open spiral around sides of tea light.
6. Pull spiral to desired length.

Etch the Glass:

1. Use the pattern provided on page 126 to cut a template from self-adhesive paper. Adhere around bottle sides.
2. Brush etching cream over the entire outer bottle and template. Allow glass to etch according to etching cream manufacturer's instructions.
3. Wash away etching cream. Remove adhesive paper patterns.

Assemble:

Slide spiraled wire with tea light candle through bottle so loop extends through top of bottle. ❏

Pattern for Frosted Wine Bottle Lantern
(actual size)

Metric Conversion Chart

Inches to Millimeters and Centimeters

Inches	MM	CM	Inches	MM	CM
1/8	3	.3	2	51	5.1
1/4	6	.6	3	76	7.6
3/8	10	1.0	4	102	10.2
1/2	13	1.3	5	127	12.7
5/8	16	1.6	6	152	15.2
3/4	19	1.9	7	178	17.8
7/8	22	2.2	8	203	20.3
1	25	2.5	9	229	22.9
1-1/4	32	3.2	10	254	25.4
1-1/2	38	3.8	11	279	27.9
1-3/4	44	4.4	12	305	30.5

Yards to Meters

Yards	Meters	Yards	Meters
1/8	.11	3	2.74
1/4	.23	4	3.66
3/8	.34	5	4.57
1/2	.46	6	5.49
5/8	.57	7	6.40
3/4	.69	8	7.32
7/8	.80	9	8.23
1	.91	10	9.14
2	1.83		

Index

Continued on next page

Index